FREE Test Taking Tips DVD Offer

To help us better serve you, we have developed a Test Taking Tips DVD that we would like to give you for FREE. **This DVD covers world-class test taking tips that you can use to be even more successful when you are taking your test.**

All that we ask is that you email us your feedback about your study guide. Please let us know what you thought about it – whether that is good, bad or indifferent.

To get your **FREE Test Taking Tips DVD**, email freedvd@studyguideteam.com with "FREE DVD" in the subject line and the following information in the body of the email:

   a. The title of your study guide.

   b. Your product rating on a scale of 1-5, with 5 being the highest rating.

   c. Your feedback about the study guide. What did you think of it?

   d. Your full name and shipping address to send your free DVD.

If you have any questions or concerns, please don't hesitate to contact us at freedvd@studyguideteam.com.

Thanks again!

AP Human Geography 2021 and 2022 Study Guide

Advanced Placement Review Book with Practice Exam Questions [3rd Edition Prep]

Joshua Rueda

Interested in buying more than 10 copies of our product? Contact us about bulk discounts:
bulkorders@studyguideteam.com

ISBN 13: 9781637751060
ISBN 10: 1637751060

 Test Prep Books!!!

Table of Contents

Quick Overview

As you draw closer to taking your exam, effective preparation becomes more and more important. Thankfully, you have this study guide to help you get ready. Use this guide to help keep your studying on track and refer to it often.

This study guide contains several key sections that will help you be successful on your exam. The guide contains tips for what you should do the night before and the day of the test. Also included are test-taking tips. Knowing the right information is not always enough. Many well-prepared test takers struggle with exams. These tips will help equip you to accurately read, assess, and answer test questions.

A large part of the guide is devoted to showing you what content to expect on the exam and to helping you better understand that content. In this guide are practice test questions so that you can see how well you have grasped the content. Then, answer explanations are provided so that you can understand why you missed certain questions.

Don't try to cram the night before you take your exam. This is not a wise strategy for a few reasons. First, your retention of the information will be low. Your time would be better used by reviewing information you already know rather than trying to learn a lot of new information. Second, you will likely become stressed as you try to gain a large amount of knowledge in a short amount of time. Third, you will be depriving yourself of sleep. So be sure to go to bed at a reasonable time the night before. Being well-rested helps you focus and remain calm.

Be sure to eat a substantial breakfast the morning of the exam. If you are taking the exam in the afternoon, be sure to have a good lunch as well. Being hungry is distracting and can make it difficult to focus. You have hopefully spent lots of time preparing for the exam. Don't let an empty stomach get in the way of success!

When travelling to the testing center, leave earlier than needed. That way, you have a buffer in case you experience any delays. This will help you remain calm and will keep you from missing your appointment time at the testing center.

Be sure to pace yourself during the exam. Don't try to rush through the exam. There is no need to risk performing poorly on the exam just so you can leave the testing center early. Allow yourself to use all of the allotted time if needed.

Remain positive while taking the exam even if you feel like you are performing poorly. Thinking about the content you should have mastered will not help you perform better on the exam.

Once the exam is complete, take some time to relax. Even if you feel that you need to take the exam again, you will be well served by some down time before you begin studying again. It's often easier to convince yourself to study if you know that it will come with a reward!

Test-Taking Strategies

1. Predicting the Answer

When you feel confident in your preparation for a multiple-choice test, try predicting the answer before reading the answer choices. This is especially useful on questions that test objective factual knowledge. By predicting the answer before reading the available choices, you eliminate the possibility that you will be distracted or led astray by an incorrect answer choice. You will feel more confident in your selection if you read the question, predict the answer, and then find your prediction among the answer choices. After using this strategy, be sure to still read all of the answer choices carefully and completely. If you feel unprepared, you should not attempt to predict the answers. This would be a waste of time and an opportunity for your mind to wander in the wrong direction.

2. Reading the Whole Question

Too often, test takers scan a multiple-choice question, recognize a few familiar words, and immediately jump to the answer choices. Test authors are aware of this common impatience, and they will sometimes prey upon it. For instance, a test author might subtly turn the question into a negative, or he or she might redirect the focus of the question right at the end. The only way to avoid falling into these traps is to read the entirety of the question carefully before reading the answer choices.

3. Looking for Wrong Answers

Long and complicated multiple-choice questions can be intimidating. One way to simplify a difficult multiple-choice question is to eliminate all of the answer choices that are clearly wrong. In most sets of answers, there will be at least one selection that can be dismissed right away. If the test is administered on paper, the test taker could draw a line through it to indicate that it may be ignored; otherwise, the test taker will have to perform this operation mentally or on scratch paper. In either case, once the obviously incorrect answers have been eliminated, the remaining choices may be considered. Sometimes identifying the clearly wrong answers will give the test taker some information about the correct answer. For instance, if one of the remaining answer choices is a direct opposite of one of the eliminated answer choices, it may well be the correct answer. The opposite of obviously wrong is obviously right! Of course, this is not always the case. Some answers are obviously incorrect simply because they are irrelevant to the question being asked. Still, identifying and eliminating some incorrect answer choices is a good way to simplify a multiple-choice question.

4. Don't Overanalyze

Anxious test takers often overanalyze questions. When you are nervous, your brain will often run wild, causing you to make associations and discover clues that don't actually exist. If you feel that this may be a problem for you, do whatever you can to slow down during the test. Try taking a deep breath or counting to ten. As you read and consider the question, restrict yourself to the particular words used by the author. Avoid thought tangents about what the author *really* meant, or what he or she was *trying* to say. The only things that matter on a multiple-choice test are the words that are actually in the question. You must avoid reading too much into a multiple-choice question, or supposing that the writer meant something other than what he or she wrote.

5. No Need for Panic

It is wise to learn as many strategies as possible before taking a multiple-choice test, but it is likely that you will come across a few questions for which you simply don't know the answer. In this situation, avoid panicking. Because most multiple-choice tests include dozens of questions, the relative value of a single wrong answer is small. As much as possible, you should compartmentalize each question on a multiple-choice test. In other words, you should not allow your feelings about one question to affect your success on the others. When you find a question that you either don't understand or don't know how to answer, just take a deep breath and do your best. Read the entire question slowly and carefully. Try rephrasing the question a couple of different ways. Then, read all of the answer choices carefully. After eliminating obviously wrong answers, make a selection and move on to the next question.

6. Confusing Answer Choices

When working on a difficult multiple-choice question, there may be a tendency to focus on the answer choices that are the easiest to understand. Many people, whether consciously or not, gravitate to the answer choices that require the least concentration, knowledge, and memory. This is a mistake. When you come across an answer choice that is confusing, you should give it extra attention. A question might be confusing because you do not know the subject matter to which it refers. If this is the case, don't eliminate the answer before you have affirmatively settled on another. When you come across an answer choice of this type, set it aside as you look at the remaining choices. If you can confidently assert that one of the other choices is correct, you can leave the confusing answer aside. Otherwise, you will need to take a moment to try to better understand the confusing answer choice. Rephrasing is one way to tease out the sense of a confusing answer choice.

7. Your First Instinct

Many people struggle with multiple-choice tests because they overthink the questions. If you have studied sufficiently for the test, you should be prepared to trust your first instinct once you have carefully and completely read the question and all of the answer choices. There is a great deal of research suggesting that the mind can come to the correct conclusion very quickly once it has obtained all of the relevant information. At times, it may seem to you as if your intuition is working faster even than your reasoning mind. This may in fact be true. The knowledge you obtain while studying may be retrieved from your subconscious before you have a chance to work out the associations that support it. Verify your instinct by working out the reasons that it should be trusted.

8. Key Words

Many test takers struggle with multiple-choice questions because they have poor reading comprehension skills. Quickly reading and understanding a multiple-choice question requires a mixture of skill and experience. To help with this, try jotting down a few key words and phrases on a piece of scrap paper. Doing this concentrates the process of reading and forces the mind to weigh the relative importance of the question's parts. In selecting words and phrases to write down, the test taker thinks about the question more deeply and carefully. This is especially true for multiple-choice questions that are preceded by a long prompt.

9. Subtle Negatives

One of the oldest tricks in the multiple-choice test writer's book is to subtly reverse the meaning of a question with a word like *not* or *except*. If you are not paying attention to each word in the question, you can easily be led astray by this trick. For instance, a common question format is, "Which of the following is…?" Obviously, if the question instead is, "Which of the following is not…?," then the answer will be quite different. Even worse, the test makers are aware of the potential for this mistake and will include one answer choice that would be correct if the question were not negated or reversed. A test taker who misses the reversal will find what he or she believes to be a correct answer and will be so confident that he or she will fail to reread the question and discover the original error. The only way to avoid this is to practice a wide variety of multiple-choice questions and to pay close attention to each and every word.

10. Reading Every Answer Choice

It may seem obvious, but you should always read every one of the answer choices! Too many test takers fall into the habit of scanning the question and assuming that they understand the question because they recognize a few key words. From there, they pick the first answer choice that answers the question they believe they have read. Test takers who read all of the answer choices might discover that one of the latter answer choices is actually *more* correct. Moreover, reading all of the answer choices can remind you of facts related to the question that can help you arrive at the correct answer. Sometimes, a misstatement or incorrect detail in one of the latter answer choices will trigger your memory of the subject and will enable you to find the right answer. Failing to read all of the answer choices is like not reading all of the items on a restaurant menu: you might miss out on the perfect choice.

11. Spot the Hedges

One of the keys to success on multiple-choice tests is paying close attention to every word. This is never truer than with words like almost, most, some, and sometimes. These words are called "hedges" because they indicate that a statement is not totally true or not true in every place and time. An absolute statement will contain no hedges, but in many subjects, the answers are not always straightforward or absolute. There are always exceptions to the rules in these subjects. For this reason, you should favor those multiple-choice questions that contain hedging language. The presence of qualifying words indicates that the author is taking special care with his or her words, which is certainly important when composing the right answer. After all, there are many ways to be wrong, but there is only one way to be right! For this reason, it is wise to avoid answers that are absolute when taking a multiple-choice test. An absolute answer is one that says things are either all one way or all another. They often include words like *every*, *always*, *best*, and *never*. If you are taking a multiple-choice test in a subject that doesn't lend itself to absolute answers, be on your guard if you see any of these words.

12. Long Answers

In many subject areas, the answers are not simple. As already mentioned, the right answer often requires hedges. Another common feature of the answers to a complex or subjective question are qualifying clauses, which are groups of words that subtly modify the meaning of the sentence. If the question or answer choice describes a rule to which there are exceptions or the subject matter is complicated, ambiguous, or confusing, the correct answer will require many words in order to be expressed clearly and accurately. In essence, you should not be deterred by answer choices that seem excessively long. Oftentimes, the author of the text will not be able to write the correct answer without

offering some qualifications and modifications. Your job is to read the answer choices thoroughly and completely and to select the one that most accurately and precisely answers the question.

13. Restating to Understand

Sometimes, a question on a multiple-choice test is difficult not because of what it asks but because of how it is written. If this is the case, restate the question or answer choice in different words. This process serves a couple of important purposes. First, it forces you to concentrate on the core of the question. In order to rephrase the question accurately, you have to understand it well. Rephrasing the question will concentrate your mind on the key words and ideas. Second, it will present the information to your mind in a fresh way. This process may trigger your memory and render some useful scrap of information picked up while studying.

14. True Statements

Sometimes an answer choice will be true in itself, but it does not answer the question. This is one of the main reasons why it is essential to read the question carefully and completely before proceeding to the answer choices. Too often, test takers skip ahead to the answer choices and look for true statements. Having found one of these, they are content to select it without reference to the question above. Obviously, this provides an easy way for test makers to play tricks. The savvy test taker will always read the entire question before turning to the answer choices. Then, having settled on a correct answer choice, he or she will refer to the original question and ensure that the selected answer is relevant. The mistake of choosing a correct-but-irrelevant answer choice is especially common on questions related to specific pieces of objective knowledge. A prepared test taker will have a wealth of factual knowledge at his or her disposal, and should not be careless in its application.

15. No Patterns

One of the more dangerous ideas that circulates about multiple-choice tests is that the correct answers tend to fall into patterns. These erroneous ideas range from a belief that B and C are the most common right answers, to the idea that an unprepared test-taker should answer "A-B-A-C-A-D-A-B-A." It cannot be emphasized enough that pattern-seeking of this type is exactly the WRONG way to approach a multiple-choice test. To begin with, it is highly unlikely that the test maker will plot the correct answers according to some predetermined pattern. The questions are scrambled and delivered in a random order. Furthermore, even if the test maker was following a pattern in the assignation of correct answers, there is no reason why the test taker would know which pattern he or she was using. Any attempt to discern a pattern in the answer choices is a waste of time and a distraction from the real work of taking the test. A test taker would be much better served by extra preparation before the test than by reliance on a pattern in the answers.

FREE DVD OFFER

Don't forget that doing well on your exam includes both understanding the test content and understanding how to use what you know to do well on the test. We offer a completely FREE Test Taking Tips DVD that covers world class test taking tips that you can use to be even more successful when you are taking your test.

All that we ask is that you email us your feedback about your study guide. To get your **FREE Test Taking Tips DVD**, email freedvd@studyguideteam.com with "FREE DVD" in the subject line and the following information in the body of the email:

- The title of your study guide.
- Your product rating on a scale of 1-5, with 5 being the highest rating.
- Your feedback about the study guide. What did you think of it?
- Your full name and shipping address to send your free DVD.

Introduction

Function of the Test

The Advanced Placement (AP) Human Geography Exam, created by the College Board, is an exam designed to offer college placement for high school students. The AP program allows students to earn college credit, advanced placement, or both, through the program's offering of the course and end-of-course exam. Sometimes universities may also look at AP scores to determine college admission. This guide gives an overview of the exam along with a condensed version of what might be taught in the AP Human Geography course.

The AP program creates multiple versions of each AP exam to be administered within various U.S. geographic regions. With these exams, schools can offer late testing and discourage sharing questions across time zones. The AP exam is given in the U.S. nationwide; and outside of Canada and the U.S., credits are only sometimes accepted in other countries. The College Board website has a list of universities outside of the U.S. that recognize AP for credit and admission.

In 2019, over 216,700 students took the AP Human Geography exam with a pass rate of 49.1%.

Test Administration

On their website, the College Board provides a specific day that the AP Human Geography exam is given. For example, in 2020, the AP Human Geography exam is given on Tuesday, May 5, at 12 p.m. Coordinators should notify students when and where to report.

Students may take the exam again if they are not happy with their results. However, since the exam is given one day per year, students must wait until the following year to retake the exam. Both scores will be reported unless the student cancels or withholds one of the scores.

A wide range of accommodations are available to students who live with disabilities. Students will work with their school to request accommodations. If students or parents do not request accommodations through their school, disabilities must be appropriately documented and requested in advance via the College Board website.

Test Format

The AP Human Geography exam is two hours and fifteen minutes long and contains a multiple-choice section and a free-response section. The multiple-choice section is made up of maps and spatial data and has sixty questions total. This section takes up 50 percent of the exam and lasts one hour. The free-response section has three parts that provides data, text, or a map and asks you to answer questions related to each part. This section takes up 50 percent of the exam and lasts for one hour and fifteen minutes.

The exam tests on human population, political systems, means of production, and differing cultures.

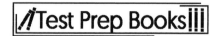

Scoring

Scoring on the AP exam is similar to that of a college course. The table below shows an outline of scores and what they mean:

Score	Recommendation	College Grade
5	Extremely well qualified	A
4	Well qualified	A-, B+,B
3	Qualified	B-,C+,C
2	Possibly qualified	n/a
1	No recommendation	n/a

While multiple-choice questions are graded via machine, free-response questions are graded by AP Readers. Scores on the free-response section are weighted and combined with the scores from the multiple-choice questions. The raw score from these two sections is converted into a 1–5 scale, as explained in the table above.

Colleges are responsible for setting their own criteria for placement and admissions, so check with specific universities to assess their criteria concerning the AP exam.

Thinking Geographically

Introduction to Maps

Types of Maps

Rather than attempting to replicate the real world, **maps** symbolically represent relationships between physical places. These symbolic representations can feature a variety of characteristics, depending on the type of map. There are two types of maps: reference maps and thematic maps. Reference maps feature a spatial representation of places, while thematic maps provide a comparison of places through the incorporation of data and relative statistics. Maps of all types provide information related to spatial patterns, including absolute distance, relative distance, and direction. Three common categories of spatial patterns are used to portray relationships on maps: point patterns, line patterns, and area patterns. These patterns portray relationships between places based on differences contained in the pattern. For example, an area pattern could differentiate between various regions' climates through the use of multiple colors or shades of the same color.

Reference Maps

Reference maps display a spatial representation of places, allowing viewers to understand the relationship between different geographical locations. There are a number of different types of reference maps, including general reference maps, topographical maps, nautical charts, and cadastral maps. **General reference maps** are the most commonly used type of map in everyday life. For example, a tourist might look at a general reference map to find where they want to go and determine how they will get there. General reference maps include both natural and manmade features, such as cities, towns, buildings, roadways, lakes, rivers, and forests. **Topographical maps** feature the relief of a landscape, including terrain's elevation, slope, and orientation. Relief is most often displayed through contour lines—lines that show relief based on curvature. Topographical maps are most often used by engineers, geologists, and outdoor adventurers. **Nautical charts** are similar to general reference maps and topographic maps except they stress the location of hazards, like submerged rocks, manmade barriers to travel, and shallow waters. In addition, nautical charts emphasize information about the coastlines, currents, magnetic fields, and tides. **Cadastral maps** are detailed maps most commonly used by land surveyors. For example, someone looking to purchase a house would view cadastral maps to identify the property's specific boundaries. The United States conducts numerous cadastral surveys to optimize land management and plan future infrastructure projects.

Thematic Maps

Thematic maps use two-dimensional surfaces to convey complex political, physical, social, cultural, economic, or historical themes. Thematic maps can be broken down into different subgroups: dot-density maps and flow-line maps. A **dot-density map** is a type of thematic map that illustrates the volume and density in a particular area. Although most dots on these maps represent the number of people in an area, they don't always have to do that. Instead, these maps may represent the number of events, such as lightning strikes, that have taken place in an area. **Flow-line maps** are another type of thematic map, which utilize both thin and thick lines to illustrate the movement of goods, people, or animals between two places. The thicker the line, the greater the number of moving elements.

Absolute and Relative Distance and Direction

Spatial patterns on maps include direction, absolute distance, and relative distance. **Direction** is most often expressed through a compass rose identifying cardinal points and intercardinal points. The cardinal points are north (N), east (E), south (S), and west (W). The **intercardinal points** are northeast (NE), southeast (SE), southwest (SW), and northwest (NW). **Absolute distance** is the physical distance between two locations as measured by a designated unit of measurement, like miles or kilometers. For example, the absolute distance between New York City and Boston is 306 kilometers. In contrast, **relative distance** measures the interconnectedness between two places based on cultural, economic, and/or social data. For example, a map of the Northeastern United States might include the relative distance between cities as expressed through the median household income in each city.

Clustering, Dispersal, and Elevation

Clustering, dispersal, and elevation are other common types of spatial patterns that appear on maps. **Clustering** patterns are typically used to express density. For example, a thematic map displaying a city's population density will have the tightest clusters around the largest neighborhoods. **Dispersal** refers to the movement of people or things across the area portrayed on the map. For example, ecologists might use a dispersal pattern to plot the speed and location of animals' breeding patterns. **Elevation** refers to a location's height as compared to sea level, and it is most commonly displayed on topographical maps using contour lines.

Distortion of Spatial Relationships

Geographers utilize a variety of maps in their study of the spatial world. Projections are maps that represent the spherical globe on a flat surface. Conformal projections attempt to preserve shape but distort size and area. For example, the most well-known projection, the **Mercator projection**, drastically distorts the size of land areas at the poles. In this particular map, Antarctica, one of the smallest continents, appears massive, while the areas closer to the equator are depicted more accurately. Other projections attempt to lessen the amount of distortion; the equal-area projection, for example, attempts to accurately represent the size of landforms. However, equal-area projections alter the shapes and angles of landforms regardless of their positioning on the map. Other projections are hybrids of the two primary models. For example, the Robinson projection tries to balance form and area in order to create a more visually accurate representation of the spatial world. Despite the efforts to maintain consistency with shapes, projections cannot provide accurate representations of the Earth's surface due to their flat, two-dimensional nature. In this sense, projections are useful symbols of space, but they do not always provide the most accurate portrayal of reality.

Unlike projections, topographic maps display contour lines, which represent the relative elevation of a particular place and are very useful for surveyors, engineers, and/or travelers. For example, hikers may refer to topographic maps to calculate their daily climbs.

Similar to topographic maps, **isoline maps** are also useful for calculating data and differentiating between the characteristics of two places. These maps use symbols to represent values and lines to connect points with the same value. For example, an isoline map could display average temperatures of a given area. The sections which share the same average temperature would be grouped together by lines. Additionally, isoline maps can help geographers study the world by generating questions. For example, is elevation the only reason for differences in temperature? If not, what other factors could cause the disparity between the values?

Thematic maps are also quite useful because they display the geographical distribution of complex political, physical, social, cultural, economic, or historical themes. For example, a thematic map could indicate an area's election results using a different color for each candidate. There are several different kinds of thematic maps, including dot-density maps and flow-line maps. A *dot-density map* uses dots to illustrate volume and density; these dots could represent a certain population, or the number of specific

events that have taken place in an area. Flow-line maps utilize lines of varying thicknesses to illustrate the movement of goods, people, or even animals between two places. Thicker lines represent a greater number of moving elements, and thinner lines represent a smaller number.

Geographic Data

Geographic Data Collection

Gathering Data

Geographic data is essential to understanding both the spatial and human realms of geography. For instance, geographers can use data and comparative analysis to determine the different factors that affect quality of life, such as population density, infant mortality rates, and literacy rates. In addition, organizations such as the **Population Reference Bureau** and the **Central Intelligence Agency** provide incredible amounts of demographic data that are readily accessible for anyone.

The **CIA World Factbook** is an indispensable resource for anyone interested in geography. Providing information about land area, literacy rates, birth rates, and economics, this resource is one of the most comprehensive on the Internet. In addition to the CIA World Factbook, the **Population Reference Bureau (PRB)** also provides students of geography with an abundant supply of information. In contrast to the CIA source, the PRB provides a treasure trove of analyses related to human populations including HIV rates, immigration rates, and poverty rates.

Furthermore, the United States Census Bureau provides similar information about the dynamics of the American population. Not only does this source focus on the data geographers need to understand the world, but it also provides information about upcoming classes, online workshops, and even includes an online library of resources for both students and teachers.

Websites for each source can be found below:

- Population Reference Bureau: www.prb.org
- United States Census Bureau: www.census.gov
- CIA World Factbook: https://www.cia.gov/library/publications/the-world-factbook/

Geospatial Technologies

Geospatial technologies are cutting-edge systems used to collect, manage, and analyze geographic data and information. The four most commonly used geospatial technologies are: geographic information systems (GIS), online mapping and visualization, remote sensing, and satellite navigation systems. Geologists mostly use **GIS technologies** to digitize data and information, particularly in terms of transferring a survey plan onto a computer. Digitization allows people to more easily view and manipulate massive amounts of data and information. GIS technologies have a number of applications, ranging from real estate development to the management of natural resources. In addition, GIS technologies often facilitate the creation of online maps and visualization projects, which allows users to interact with precise models of complex natural phenomenon.

Remote sensing refers to the collection of information without firsthand observation, which enables data acquisition to occur across considerable distances. Scientists typically conduct remote sensing with satellites and aircrafts equipped with technology capable of collecting data from the land, water, and atmosphere. Data acquired through remote sensing is often fed into GIS technologies to create online maps and visualizations, and remote sensing is regularly used across all Earth science disciplines, like ecology and geology. **Satellite navigation systems** deploy a system of satellites to automatically provide geo-spatial information to compatible electronic receivers, which allows users to determine their location with incredible precision. In addition to providing information on the receivers' longitude, latitude, altitude, and elevation, satellites' signals calculate the local time, resulting in accurate time synchronization. As of 2019, the United States and Russia are the only countries with fully developed global navigation satellite systems, meaning the satellites can collect location data from anywhere in the world. The system in the United States is called GPS, and Russia's is GLONASS.

Where Spatial Information Comes From

While remote sensing accounts for the overwhelming bulk of spatial data acquisition, information is also collected from a variety of non-technological sources. **Field observations** are the acquisition of data from firsthand accounts of geographic locations. Media reports provide a range of spatial information, including firsthand accounts, statistics, and expert analysis. Policy documents are generally written by professionals with subject matter expertise, typically at the behest of a government, corporation, or nonprofit organization. Personal interviews facilitate the collection of geographic data and information from people with firsthand knowledge or subject matter expertise. Landscape analysis is the study of how a geographic area interacts with plate tectonics, climate conditions, human development, and other relevant factors. Photographic interpretations allow experts to collect data without personally visiting the location, and the analysis typically includes a comparison of photographs from the same location at different times.

The Power of Geographic Data

Geographical Effects of Decisions Made Using Geographical Information

The application of geographical information has wide-ranging consequences, depending on the purpose of the analysis and its ultimate conclusion. Some of the most negative geographical effects occur when corporations and governments apply geographical information to exploit natural resources, leading to levels of unsustainable consumption and the devastation of entire ecosystems. On the other hand, corporations and governments have applied geographical information to limit consumption, promote sustainable human development, and preserve immense geographical areas, such as the U.S. National Forests.

Geospatial and Geographical Data are Used at all Scales

Geospatial and geographical data have a wide range of commercial, governmental, organizational, and personal applications. **Census data** is the lynchpin for democracies because it ensures that representation in government mirrors population trends. Businesses also use census data to evaluate markets. For example, if the census demonstrates population growth, then a business might expand its operations to capture the expanding market before competitors do. Satellites have revolutionized communication and transportation, especially in improving mobile technologies and increasing the internet's ability to present information about places and events in real time. Consequently, people and businesses can share information and navigate their environment with unprecedented efficiency. Many governments also use geographic data obtained through satellite imagery to detect everything from natural disasters to the manufacturing of nuclear weapons. Geospatial and geographical data also increase the efficiency of natural resource extraction and the delivery of governmental services. In theory, this increased efficiency should facilitate more sustainable development, but it often leads to the unprecedented extraction and consumption of natural resources.

Spatial Concepts

<u>Major Geographic Concepts that Illustrate Spatial Relationships</u>
Absolute and Relative Location
Location is the central theme in understanding spatial concepts. In geography, there are two primary types of location: relative and absolute. Relative location involves locating objects by their proximity to another object. For example, a person giving directions may refer to well-known landmarks, highways, or intersections along the route to provide a better frame of reference. Absolute location is the exact latitudinal and longitudinal position on the globe. A common way of identifying **absolute location** is through the use of digital, satellite-based technologies such as **GPS (Global Positioning System),** which uses sensors that interact with satellites orbiting the Earth. Coordinates correspond with positions on a manmade grid system using imaginary lines known as latitude (also known as parallels) and longitude (also known as meridians).

Lines of latitude run parallel to the *Equator* and measure distance from north to south. Lines of longitude run parallel to the *Prime Meridian* and measure distance from east to west.

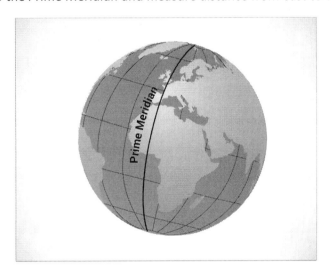

The Equator and the Prime Meridian serve as anchors of the grid system and create the basis for absolute location. They also divide the Earth into **hemispheres**. The **equator** divides the Earth into the northern and southern hemispheres, while the **Prime Meridian** establishes the eastern and western hemispheres. Lines of latitude are measured by degrees from 0 at the Equator to 90 at the North and South Poles. Lines of longitude are measured by degrees from 0 at the Prime Meridian to 180 at the International Date Line. Coordinates are used to express a specific location using its latitude and longitude and are always expressed in the following format: degree north or south followed by degree east or west (for example, 40°N, 50°E). Since there is great distance between lines of latitude and longitude, absolute locations are often found in between two lines. In those cases, degrees are broken down into minutes and seconds, which are expressed in this manner: (40° 53' 44" N, 50° 22' 65" E).

In addition to the equator and the Prime Meridian, other major lines of latitude and longitude exist to divide the world into regions relative to the direct rays of the sun. These lines correspond with the **Earth's tilt,** and are responsible for the seasons. For example, the northern hemisphere is tilted directly toward the sun from June 22 to September 23, which creates the summer season in that part of the world. Conversely, the southern hemisphere is tilted away from the direct rays of the sun and experiences winter during those same months.

The area between the **Tropic of Cancer** and the **Tropic of Capricorn** (called the tropics) has more direct exposure to the sun, tends to be warmer year-round, and experiences fewer variations in seasonal temperatures. Most of the Earth's population lives in the area between the Tropic of Cancer and the Arctic Circle (66.5 degrees north), which is one of the middle latitudes. In the Southern Hemisphere, the middle latitudes exist between the Tropic of Capricorn and the Antarctic Circle (66.5 degrees south). In both of these places, indirect rays of the sun strike the Earth. Therefore, seasons are more pronounced, and milder temperatures generally prevail. The final region, known as the **high latitudes**, is found north of the Arctic Circle and south of the Antarctic Circle. These regions generally tend to be cold all year, and experience nearly twenty-four hours of sunlight during their respective **summer solstice** and twenty-four hours of darkness during the **winter solstice**.

Seasons in the Southern Hemispheres are opposite of those in the Northern Hemisphere due to the position of the Earth as it rotates around the sun. An **equinox** occurs when the sun's rays are directly over the Equator, and day and night are of almost equal length throughout the world. Equinoxes occur twice a year. The fall, or autumnal equinox, occurs on September 22nd, while the spring equinox occurs on March 20th. If seasons are opposite of one another depending on the hemisphere, the corresponding names flip-flop depending on one's location. For example, when the Northern Hemisphere is experiencing summer, it is winter in the Southern Hemisphere.

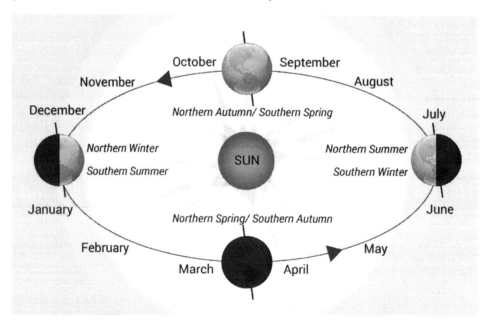

Place
While absolute and relative location identify where something is, the concept of place identifies the distinguishing physical and human characteristics of specific locations. People use **toponyms**, names of locations, to define and further orient themselves with their sense of place. Toponyms may be derived from geographical features, important historical figures in the area, or even wildlife commonly found there. For example, many cities in the state of Texas are named in honor of military leaders who fought in the Texas Revolution (such as Houston and Austin), while Mississippi and Alabama got their toponyms from Native American words.

Regions
Geographers divide the world into regions to help them understand differences inherent within the world, its people, and its environment. As mentioned previously, lines of latitude and longitude divide

the Earth into solar regions relative to the amount of sunlight they receive. Additionally, geographers identify formal and functional regions.

Formal regions are spatially defined areas that have overarching similarities or some level of homogeneity or uniformity. A formal region generally has at least one characteristic that is consistent throughout the entire area. For example, the United States could be classified as one massive formal region because English is the primary language spoken in all fifty states. Even more specifically, the United States is a linguistic region—a place where everyone generally speaks the same language.

Functional regions are areas that also have similar characteristics but do not have clear boundaries. Large cities and their metropolitan areas form functional regions, as people from outside the official city limit must travel into the city regularly for work, entertainment, restaurants, etc. Other determining factors of a functional region could be a sports team, a school district, or a shopping center. For example, New York City has two professional baseball, basketball, and football teams. As a result, its citizens may have affinities for different teams even though they live in the same city. Conversely, a citizen in rural Idaho may cheer for the Seattle Seahawks, even though they live over 500 miles from Seattle.

Space, Flows, Distant Decay, Time-Space Compression, and Pattern

Some of the most critical spatial concepts in geography include space, flows, distance decay, time-space compression, and pattern. **Space** is an abstract concept that functions as the foundation for human geography. In general, space involves the relationship between the natural environment, places, and all entities interacting within some designated place. Expressed another way, space is what geographers attempt to map, organize, and analyze. **Distance decay** refers to the impact that distance has on the interrelatedness of two locations. As the distance increases, the intensity and frequency of interactions statistically decrease. Technology has mitigated some of distance decay's impact. The invention of railroad systems, telegraphs, telephones, radios, airplanes, cell phones, and the internet have all caused a decline in distance decay. **Time-space compression** is a spatial concept related to increased speeds of travel through physical and digital space. All the inventions listed above have increased the rate of time-space compression.

Flows involve the movement of people, animals, plants, goods, capital, culture, or information in between places through time and space. Therefore, flows represent the degree of connection between places, with stronger flows indicating a higher degree of interconnectedness. Flows are not always symmetrical between two places. In particular, outgoing cultural flows tend to originate from the wealthiest and most powerful countries. For example, contemporary cultural flows from the United States to other countries are generally much greater than any single country's cultural flows to the United States. Flows can also be understood as patterns of interaction between geographic places. Patterns involve the structure, arrangement, and/or movement of people or entities. Geographers look for patterns to understand spatial relationships. In general, the most significant patterns are repetitive, consistent, and/or self-evident. Patterns are most easily recognized by plotting data on a map, especially when the data presents a cluster (high concentration) or indicates some directional movement.

Human-Environmental Interaction

How Major Geographic Concepts Illustrate Spatial Relationships

Major geographic concepts provide information about spatial relationships. Location includes both absolute and relative location, and it provides the foundation for spatial comparisons between different places. Regions group locations together on the basis of a shared characteristic or pattern of activity, and this concept helps to organize analyses of spatial relationships. Density and dispersion help geographers to understand the past, present, and future relative position of entities within a geographic area. Size and scale allow geographers to symbolize complex spatial relationships on a map or other visual medium, which facilitates a deeper analysis.

Sustainability, Natural Resources, and Land Use

Concepts of nature and society inform the development of human societies and their impact on the environment. **Land use** refers to how humans modify and manage the natural environment, particularly in terms of transforming wilderness into settlements and agricultural areas. Inefficient and exploitive land use has strained human societies since the dawn of time, and it has and even triggered their collapse. **Sustainability** is the key to optimizing land use and averting disaster. Sustainable development occurs when human societies harness the power of ecosystems and natural resources for human use without depleting or destroying the environment. Natural resources are especially critical for societies to survive and thrive. Examples of natural resources include clean air, freshwater, heavy metals (gold, iron, silver, etc.), animals, plants, minerals, timber, and fossil fuels (petroleum, coal, and natural gas).

Environmental Determinism to Possibilism

There is an ongoing controversy amongst social scientists over the interactions between natural environments and the development of human societies. Since ancient times, scholars have hypothesized that the environment could influence, and even determine, personal and societal characteristics. This view about the primacy of environment is called **environmental determinism**. However, environmental determinism is often criticized for downplaying the impact of cultural, economic, political, and social conditions. In addition, environmental determinism has been historically used to justify colonialism, Eurocentrism, and white supremacy. For example, Thomas Jefferson argued that colonialism and slavery actually benefited African people because warm weather created societies that were plagued with laziness and degeneracy. Adolf Hitler also infamously used environmental determinism to elevate the Aryan race above all others.

During the latter half of the 20th century, **environmental possibilism** has overtaken environmental determinism in terms of acceptance within the scientific community. Environmental possibilism concedes that nature places constraints on societal development, but it asserts that humanity's intelligence has allowed societies to overcome those limits. Furthermore, scholars adhering to environmental possibilism believe that culture is far more related to social and political conditions than geographical factors. In recent years, there has been some pushback against environmental possibilism due to the emergence of neo-environmental determinism. In contrast to its predecessor theory, **neo-environmental determinism** doesn't contend that geography and climate fully determine the development of society, but it does emphasize the physical environment's impact on societies. Jared Diamond's bestselling book *Guns, Germs, and Steel* is credited with popularizing neo-environmental determinism amongst the broader public, but some social scientists have disputed his claims, particularly his explanation of economic growth disparities based on environmental factors.

Scales of Analysis

Scales of Analysis Used by Geographers

Unlike the typical scales on a map, which provide information about how distance or characteristics are symbolized, **scales of analysis** enable a spatial comparison of a particular characteristic. For example, a scale of analysis could be used to analyze the gross domestic product (GDP) of European countries. Scales of analysis provide relative benchmarks for analysis. In other words, a particular characteristic can

easily be compared to its prevalence in surrounding or even distant regions, depending on the scale of analysis that's used.

Scales of Analysis Include Global, Regional, National, and Local

Geographers use a variety of scales of analysis to interpret geospatial and quantitative data. From largest to smallest, the different types of scales of analysis are: global, regional, national, and local scales. A **global scale of analysis** is incredibly broad, covering the entire Earth. Given its breadth, a global scale of analysis is typically used to discover and analyze general patterns for common characteristics, such as economic growth and climate. A **regional scale of analysis** can range dramatically in size and scope, depending on how the geographer defines a region. For example, geographers could use a regional scale that covers Afro-Eurasia, Europe, or Northwestern Europe. A **national scale of analysis** is the most specific variant because it's used to interpret data within a country's boundaries, which are formally defined. A **local scale of analysis** is most often used to study cities. However, this type of analysis can also be hyper-localized, focusing on a specific neighborhood or city block.

What Scales of Analysis Reveal

Scales of analysis are useful because the spatial comparison provides context for interpretation, revealing patterns and processes. As a result, geographers can better determine how certain variables impact a region or the relationship between regions. Scales of analysis are regularly used by geographers to interpret the effects of natural events, government policies, and cultural shifts. Additionally, scales of analysis can help geographers forecast future developments by highlighting the similarities in conditions and/or characteristics between two locations.

Patterns and Processes at Different Scales Reveal Variations in Data

Scales of analysis are particularly useful for quantitative data, such as population density or economic variables. However, scales of analysis can also be used to interpret geospatial data, visual imagery, and geographic characteristics, like topographical landscapes. Geospatial data is particularly important due to the sheer volume of data that's available. For example, governments, corporations, and nonprofits collect massive amounts of geospatial data on transportation networks, water usage, climate changes, economic exchanges, and a multitude of other variables. In turn, this data can be manipulated and interpreted at different scales to yield information about the past, present, and future state of a geographic area.

Regional Analysis

How Geographers Define Regions

Geographers define regions based on a characteristic that's shared across a designated geographic area, and, in general, regions can be categorized as formal, functional, or perceptual/vernacular. Since defining a region is largely a subjective process, regional boundaries tend to be transitional and can overlap. Furthermore, regional boundaries are regularly the subject of disputes due to cultural or political reasons. Geographers sometimes use global, national, and local scales to get a firm understanding of the context behind a region's past, present, and future trends.

Definition of Regions

Regions can be classified in a variety of ways, though each definition typically involves a unifying characteristic or common pattern of activity. One of the most common unifying characteristics is culture, including food, language, religion, traditions, and values. In addition, a region can be defined by a shared pattern of economic activity, such as a common agricultural practice or the presence of a dominant crop across the region. Transportation networks can also help form a region as people and locations become more interconnected. Aside from formalized political and administrative regions, some regions develop out of a common geopolitical value to other entities. For example, the Middle East is partially considered a cohesive region due to global powers' longstanding interest in its natural resources and strategic location between Europe and Asia. In fact, many American foreign policy experts refer to the entire Middle East as "the region."

Types of Regions

Regions can be broadly classified as formal, functional, and perceptual. **Formal regions** can be either manmade or defined by natural features, but they always have defined boundaries. For manmade formal regions, a government is typically the entity that defines the region. For example, in countries like the United States and Canada, it is not uncommon for schools, workplaces, or communities to have people of Asian, African, Caucasian, European, Indian, or Native descent.

In less developed parts of the world, travel is limited due to the lack of infrastructure. Consequently, ethnic groups develop in small areas that can differ greatly from other people just a few miles away. For example, on the Balkan Peninsula in southeastern Europe, a variety of different ethnic groups live in close proximity to one another. Croats, Albanians, Serbs, Bosnians, and others all share the same land but have very different worldviews, traditions, and religious influences. Unfortunately, this diversity has not always been a positive characteristic, such as when Bosnia was the scene of a horrible genocide against Albanians in an "ethnic cleansing" effort that continued throughout the late 20th century.

Linguistics

Linguistics, or the study of language, groups certain languages together according to their commonalities. For example, the Romance languages—French, Spanish, Italian, Romanian, and Portuguese—all share language traits from Latin. These languages, also known as **vernaculars**, or more commonly spoken **dialects**, evolved over centuries of physical isolation on the European continent. The Spanish form of Latin emerged into today's Spanish language. Similarly, the Bantu people of Africa travelled extensively and spread their language, now called Swahili, which became the first Pan-African language. Since thousands of languages exist, it is important to have a widespread means of communication that can interconnect people from different parts of the world. One way to do this is through a lingua franca, or a common language used for business, diplomacy, and other cross-national relationships. English is a primary lingua franca around the world, but there are many others in use as well.

Religion

Religion has played a tremendous role in creating the world's cultures. Devout Christians crossed the Atlantic in hopes of finding religious freedom in New England, Muslim missionaries and traders travelled to the Spice Islands of the East Indies to teach about the Koran, and Buddhist monks traversed the Himalayan Mountains into Tibet to spread their faith. In some countries, religion helps to shape legal systems. These nations, termed **theocracies**, have no separation of church and state and are more common in Islamic nations such as Saudi Arabia, Iran, and Qatar. In contrast, even though religion has played a tremendous role in the history of the United States, its government remains **secular**, or nonreligious, due to the influence of European Enlightenment philosophy at the time of its inception. Like ethnicity and language, religion is a primary way that individuals and people groups self-identify. As a result, religious influences can shape a region's laws, architecture, literature, and music. For example, when the Ottoman Turks, who are Muslim, conquered Constantinople, which was once the home of the Eastern Orthodox Christian Church, they replaced Christian places of worship with mosques.

Additionally, they replaced different forms of Roman architecture with those influenced by Arabic traditions.

Economics

Economic activity also has a spatial component. For example, nations with few natural resources tend to import what they need from nations willing to export raw materials. Furthermore, areas that are home to certain raw materials generally tend to alter their environment in order to maintain production of those materials. In the San Joaquin Valley of California, an area known for extreme heat and desert-like conditions, local residents have engineered elaborate drip irrigation systems to adequately water lemon, lime, olive, and orange trees, utilizing the warm temperatures to constantly produce citrus fruits. Additionally, other nations with abundant petroleum reserves build elaborate infrastructures in order to pump, house, refine, and transport their materials to nations who require gasoline, diesel, or natural gas. Essentially, inhabitants of different spatial regions on Earth create jobs, infrastructure, and transportation systems to ensure the continued flow of goods, raw materials, and resources out of their location so long as financial resources keep flowing into the area.

Types of Diffusion

Cultural diffusion is how traits, beliefs, values, and other cultural characteristics spread between cultures. There are two primary types of cultural diffusion: relocation and expansion. Relocation diffusion is the spread of cultural traits through people moving into new areas. At times, **relocation diffusion** can shift the center of power for that cultural trait. So, relocation diffusion closely follows migration patterns.

In contrast, **expansion diffusion** occurs when a cultural trait develops and moves to new areas without losing strength in its region of origin. Therefore, the easiest way to differentiate between relocation diffusion and expansion diffusion is whether the cultural trait spread merely through people permanently resettling in new areas. If the cultural trait did *not* spread through the mere movement of people but occurred in some other way, then it's likely expansion diffusion.

There are three different types of expansion diffusion: contagious, hierarchical, and stimulus expansion. Expansion diffusion can occur between different cultures or among people within one culture. **Contagious diffusion** refers to when a cultural trait spontaneously and rapidly spreads between people, usually through direct contact. This typically occurs within a single population, but contagious diffusion can also spread across a region. **Hierarchical diffusion** is the spread of a cultural trait from large to small locations, such as cities to villages. Additionally, hierarchical diffusion often involves social elites popularizing and spreading the cultural trait. **Stimulus diffusion** occurs when the cultural trait transforms after its spread. Often, the adaption of the cultural trait makes it more popular or accessible in its new homeland.

Historical Causes of Diffusion

How Historical Processes Impact Current Cultural Patterns

Historical processes impact current cultural practices through diffusion. Trade between different cultures led to the formation of many lingua franca languages to bridge the communication divide. Military conquests, colonization, and imperialism have allowed global powers to impose their cultures on native populations. Creolization is an example of an enduring cultural pattern that developed due to colonization.

Interactions Between and Among Cultural Traits

Cultural interactions and global forces have resulted in **syncretism**, meaning the combination of cultural traits into a unique new form of cultural expression. Creolization and lingua franca are examples of syncretic cultural expression. **Creolization** refers to the combination of European, African, and indigenous cultures in the Americas during and after the colonial period. From 1500 to the present day, more than one hundred creole languages have been created. Most of these languages use English, French, or Spanish as their foundation and then incorporate vocabulary and phonetic aspects of indigenous and African languages. Creole cultures primarily developed in the American South, the Caribbean, and Brazil. The development of jazz in New Orleans is an example of creole culture. Other examples include creole religions, such as Haitian Voodoo and Cuban Santeria.

Lingua franca is an umbrella term for languages used to communicate between different cultures. Some of these languages are pre-existing, while others are pidgin languages explicitly created to facilitate basic communication. French continues to function as a lingua franca in many African countries due to the legacy of French imperialism. **Pidgin languages** are a simplified form of communication, though they can develop into more complex languages. For example, creole language developed from pidgin languages.

Colonialism, Imperialism, and Trade

Global patterns of interaction heavily influence the spread and practice of culture. In modern history, the three most important global patterns of interaction with a cultural impact are colonialism, imperialism, and free trade. All three patterns are hierarchical, meaning the more powerful society has a greater influence on the exchange.

Colonialism had the greatest effect in the Americas, especially in terms of European countries intentionally suppressing and eradicating indigenous cultures. European powers adopted **imperialist foreign policies** in the late 19th and early 20th century, and colonialism had a similarly coercive effect on native cultures in Africa and Asia. **Trade** has produced patterns of cultural exchange since ancient times, but after World War II, the expansion of global free trade intensified those patterns. While free trade is less coercive than imperialism and colonialism, it can still result in the elevation of highly developed countries' cultures above all others due to their disproportionate political and economic power.

Contemporary Causes of Diffusion

How Historical Processes Impact Current Cultural Patterns

Small-scale and large-scale historical processes have influenced cultural development. Generally speaking, **small-scale processes** impact the development of individual cultural traits, while **large-scale processes** have a widespread impact, shifting cultural foundations. Communication technologies have accelerated and amplified the effect of all these processes. In particular, the internet has created a global platform for near-instantaneous cultural diffusion in a digital space.

Urbanization and Globalization

Culture is a social construct. It's the product of human perspectives, knowledge accumulation, interpersonal interactions, and socioeconomic conditions. Consequently, small-scale and large-scale processes can play a critical role in transforming culture through economics, media, politics, technology, and social relationships. Small-scale processes with a cultural impact include fashion trends, technological innovations, and culinary movements.

Isolated small-scale processes can combine to form large-scale processes. For example, small-scale patterns of movement can increase population densities and lead to the large-scale process of

urbanization. As a result, the growing complexity of urban economic, political, and social relationships has spurred more frequent and deeper cultural interactions. Another example of a large-scale process is **globalization**, the rise of an integrated global economy. Overall, globalization has increased the interaction between different cultures, leading to more immigration, economic exchanges, transnational political structures, and cultural diffusion.

Communication Technologies

Communication technologies have altered and expedited cultural exchanges. At the end of the 20th century, the internet began allowing users to send near-instantaneous messages to anyone in the world on a variety of platforms, including social media. Furthermore, the internet functions as a massive warehouse of information. It provides unprecedented opportunities for people to learn about and interact with different cultures. Due to its extreme interconnectivity, the internet has quickened the pace of time-space convergence, meaning it takes less time to communicate across space.

The internet has had a number of direct cultural effects. Since American and British engineers played a major role in developing the internet, English was its original language. Consequently, English has become a lingua franca on the internet. The internet has also contributed to cultural convergence, particularly through the creation of a global popular culture. However, this convergence has disproportionately emphasized Western culture. Consequently, relatively rare cultural traits, like indigenous languages, have declined because they are generally excluded from the ascendant global popular culture. At the same time, the internet has led to some cultural divergence as different cultures become more segregated in the digital space. For example, the Chinese government regulates and censors the internet to such an extreme degree that it's effectively an entirely different digital space.

Diffusion of Religion and Language

Diffusion of Universalizing and Ethnic Religions

Several factors influenced the diffusion of universalizing and ethnic religions. While both universalizing and ethnic religions spread through relocation diffusion, universalizing also spread through expansion diffusion. As a result, most universalizing religions spread to a significantly greater extent than **ethnic religions**. Doctrinal differences help explain why universalizing religions embraced expansion diffusion. **Universalizing religions** believe they hold a universal truth, so they are directly applicable to everyone. In addition, several universalizing religions reward followers for proselytizing, including Christianity and Islam. Other relevant factors to the diffusion of universalizing religions include connections to commerce and military conquests.

Cultural Hearths

Cultural hearths are geographic areas where a unique culture developed. Geographers have identified seven ancient cultural hearths that developed between 4,000 and 12,000 years ago, and they were located in China, East India, Indo-Pakistan, the Fertile Crescent (Middle East), Ethiopia, Mexico, and Peru. Of these hearths, the Fertile Crescent is the oldest by approximately 5,000 years. All seven hearths were a direct result of societies' domestication of plants and animals. For example, the Fertile Crescent hearth developed after the domestication of barley, chickpeas, dates, lentils, and wheat. As agricultural production expanded, populations increased, and the cultural hearths flourished.

All the ancient cultural hearths developed languages, dialects, religions, ethnic cultures, and gender roles. Nearly all modern European languages and some Asian languages developed from the Proto-Indo-European language family, and it was spread across the Fertile Crescent and Indo-Pakistan hearths between 4500 and 2500 B.C.E., though historical projections vary. The Fertile Crescent hearth is also notable for giving birth to the two world religions with the most modern followers—Christianity and Islam. Additionally, the world's third largest religion, Hinduism, was originally established in the Indo-Pakistan hearth. Cultural traits primarily diffused from these hearths through economic exchanges and migration patterns, and over time, new hearths developed across the world.

Diffusion of Language Families

Geographers represent the diffusion of language families, religious patterns, and religious distributions in a number of ways. Maps are the most straightforward tool used to plot language and religious data. A clear legend is critical for these types of maps because detailed symbols are typically required to illustrate linguistic and religious developments, especially over long periods of time. Maps are more often used to represent religious patterns and distributions because this data is easier to plot in space. Geographers also commonly use charts in linguistic and religious analyses. For example, geographers sometimes use a chart that resembles a family tree to trace the history and connections between the hundreds of languages in the Indo-European language family. **Toponyms** are visualizations that chart how the names of places develop over time, and they can be useful in tracing the development of language families. Digital representations have been increasingly used, especially when geographers need to project the most likely series of events when there's a gap in the historical record.

Practices and Belief Systems Relating to Religion Diffusion

Religions developed in distinct locations, and they spread through different types of diffusion, depending on their practices and belief systems. Universalizing religions have historically spread by expansion diffusion and relocation diffusion. The defining characteristic of universal religions is a claim to universal truth. Therefore, universalizing religions don't exclusively appeal to any single culture or confine their religious practice to any single region. In contrast, ethnic religions don't assert a universal truth that is applicable to all people. Instead, ethnic religions typically remain near the hearth—near their place of origin—because they are less concerned with expanding than universalizing religions. However, some ethnic religions have spread away from the hearth via relocation diffusion.

Expansion diffusion has allowed universalizing religions to spread to more distant locations and gain significantly more followers than most ethnic religions. For example, Christianity and Judaism both developed in the Fertile Crescent hearth, but expansion diffusion facilitated Christianity's explosive global growth pattern. Today, there are approximately 2.4 billion Christians and 14.5 million Jews. Universalizing religion's practices and belief systems also tend to explicitly facilitate their expansion. For example, Islam and Christianity both encourage followers to engage in proselytizing as a means of spiritual growth.

Universalizing Religions

Universalizing religions have experienced tremendous growth because they are spread through both expansion diffusion and relocation diffusion. These dual patterns of diffusion have led to tremendous growth as evidenced by more than 60 percent of the world's population practicing a universalizing religion. Examples of universalizing religions include Buddhism, Christianity, Islam, and Sikhism.

Buddhism developed between the 6th and 4th century B.C.E. on the Indian subcontinent, and it spread across Central Asia, Southeast Asia, and East Asia from 250 B.C.E. onward through expansion and relocation diffusion. Specifically, Buddhism spread through stimulus diffusion as the religion spread through its connection to commerce. **Christianity** originated in Judea at the end of the 1st century B.C.E., and it has since become the only world religion to establish a significant presence on every continent. Christianity rapidly spread through relocation diffusion and contagious diffusion, and Christian

countries' colonization and sponsorship of missionaries in the Americas and Africa also spurred hierarchical diffusion. **Islam** developed in the 7th century C.E., and it rapidly spread across the Middle East and Africa. Like Christianity, the spread of Islam benefited from large-scale military conquests and missionary work. **Sikhism** originally developed on the Indian subcontinent in the late 15th century, and it spread across that continent through contagious diffusion, particularly amongst groups that opposed the Muslim Mughal Empire.

Ethnic Religions

Ethnic religions only spread through relocation diffusion, so they generally remain most popular in the immediate area surrounding the hearth. As a result, ethnic religions have considerably fewer global followers than universalizing religions. Approximately 24 percent of the world's population practices an ethnic religion, with Hinduism accounting for the overwhelming majority of total followers.

Hinduism developed on the Indian subcontinent through a syncretic blending of ancient Vedic religious practices between the 6th century B.C.E. and the 3rd century C.E. Hinduism spread to Southeast Asia between the 1st and 5th century C.E. through relocation diffusion. Other ethnic religions include Judaism, Taoism, and Confucianism. **Judaism** originally developed in Judea during the 5th century B.C.E. Judaism has spread across the Middle East, Europe, and the Americas through relocation diffusion, including forced expulsions. **Confucianism** and **Taoism** both developed in China during the Hundred Schools of Thought (6th century–221 B.C.E.). Aside from some limited relocation diffusion, the overwhelming majority of adherents to Confucianism and Taoism live in China.

Effects of Diffusion

Process of Diffusion Results in Changes to the Cultural Landscape

Diffusion affects a cultural landscape in several ways. The arrival of new cultural groups can produce changes to the population's religious and linguistic composition. Similarly, interactions between cultures can diversify economic activities, architectural styles, land use practices, and other forms of cultural expression that have an impact on the natural environment. Additionally, diffusion generally results from increased immigration, which increases population density. This can result in more urbanization, consumption, and pollution, which can alter or harm the natural environment.

Acculturation, Assimilation, Syncretism, and Multiculturalism

Cultural diffusion results in acculturation, assimilation, multiculturalism, and syncretism. **Acculturation** occurs as minority cultures socially and psychologically adapt to the majority culture. Often, acculturation results in changes to cultural preferences and practices in regards to clothing, food, language, and religion; however, the minority culture typically survives as a distinct subculture. **Assimilation** describes a process in which minority culture transforms and becomes increasingly similar to the majority culture. Unlike acculturation, assimilation commonly results in the erosion of the minority culture as a distinct group.

Syncretism is the blending of different cultural practices or beliefs into a new form of cultural expression. For example, during the late 16th century, the Mughal emperor Akbar led the development of a syncretic religion known as Din-i Ilahi to unify his empire's religiously diverse population. Din-i Ilahi combined aspects of Christianity, Islam, Hinduism, Jainism, and Zoroastrianism. Syncretism can also occur spontaneously in the absence of hierarchical direction, especially during periods of large-scale immigration. **Multiculturalism** occurs when multiple distinct cultures exist and enjoy considerable influence within a society.

Practice Questions

1. Which of the following is NOT a characteristic of cultural landscapes?
   a. Ethnocentrism
   b. Industrial practices
   c. Land use patterns
   d. Physical features
   e. Sequent occupancy

Questions 2–3 refer to the chart below.

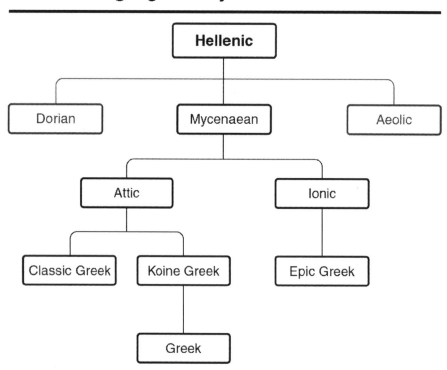

2. Which pair of languages likely shares the closest relationship in terms of linguistic characteristics?
   a. Aeolic and Greek
   b. Dorian and Classical Greek
   c. Epic Greek and Greek
   d. Ionic and Epic Greek
   e. Mycenaean and Aeolic

3. Which region is most likely the Hellenic language family's hearth region of origin?
   a. Fertile Crescent
   b. Indo-Pakistan
   c. Mediterranean Basin
   d. Mexico
   e. Peru

4. Which statement best describes the difference between cultural relativism and ethnocentrism?

a. Cultural relativism assesses the relative superiority of a culture, while ethnocentrism places more weight on a population's ethnic composition.

b. Cultural relativism emphasizes descriptive comparisons, while ethnocentrism asserts more value judgments.

c. Cultural relativism has a strong association with xenophobia, while ethnocentrism is more critical of some cultural traits.

d. Cultural relativism is most concerned with cultural traits, while ethnocentrism primarily analyzes the relationship between ethnicity and culture.

e. Cultural relativism attempts to objectively evaluate cultures, while ethnocentrism readily admits that cultural analysis is highly subjective.

Questions 5–7 refer to the map below.

South America (1776)

5. Which cultural interaction is depicted on the map?
   a. Colonialism
   b. Contagious diffusion
   c. Free trade regions
   d. Imperialism
   e. Syncretism

6. Which statement most accurately describes the immediate impact of cultural interactions between European and South American civilizations?
   a. European civilizations attempted to spread multiculturalism in South America.
   b. South American civilizations strenuously opposed the development of syncretic belief systems.
   c. South American civilizations primarily hoped to increase trade with European civilizations.
   d. South American civilizations feared interacting with European civilizations due to the threat of stimulus diffusion.
   e. European civilizations sought to eradicate indigenous cultures through coercion and violence.

7. How did Christianity primarily spread in South America during the time period represented on the map?
   a. Contagious diffusion
   b. Facilitated diffusion
   c. Hierarchical diffusion
   d. Relocation diffusion
   e. Stimulus diffusion

8. Which example best illustrates contagious diffusion?
   a. Local townspeople attend a witch trial, and a mass hysteria sweeps across the region.
   b. Muslim immigrants settle in the United States and establish a new mosque in their neighborhood.
   c. A feudal lord forces local peasants to convert to Protestantism under penalty of death.
   d. A fast food chain creates more vegetarian options prior to its highly anticipated expansion into the lucrative Indian market.
   e. A new style of music becomes popular in a large city, and several months later it can be heard all across the nearby suburbs.

9. Which of the following is an ethnic religion?
   a. Buddhism
   b. Christianity
   c. Hinduism
   d. Islam
   e. Sikhism

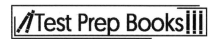

Question 10 refers to the map below.

Ancient Cultural Hearths (2,000 B.C.E.)

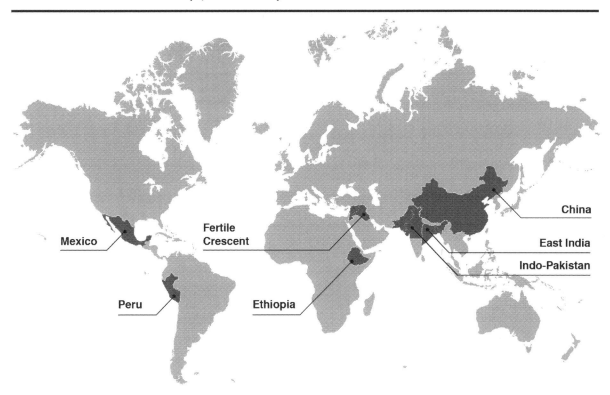

10. Which statement about the shared characteristics of the ancient cultural hearths depicted on the map is true?
   a. The hearths industrialized at a faster rate than any other region.
   b. The hearths developed based on the domestication of plants and animals.
   c. The hearths all gave birth to a universalizing religion.
   d. The hearths all developed languages that can be traced back to the Indo-European language family.
   e. The hearths all faced similar socioeconomic challenges due to their aging populations.

11. Which of the following best describes how culture is transmitted across society?
   a. Culture is almost always transmitted through hierarchical relationships, and it has a trickle-down effect.
   b. Culture is primarily transmitted through religion, economic activities, and government policies.
   c. Cultural exchanges on the internet have given rise to a global popular culture in recent years.
   d. Culture can be transmitted through an endless variety of activities, and the transmission can either be intentional or spontaneous.
   e. Given the wide variety of cultural factors, culture is impossible to define, and tracing its historical development is nearly as difficult.

12. Which of the following pairs accurately matches a world religion with the cultural hearth where it originated?
    a. Buddhism and Central Asia
    b. Christianity and Western Europe
    c. Hinduism and Southeast Asia
    d. Islam and Eastern Europe
    e. Sikhism and South Asia

Questions 13–14 refer to the table below.

Religious Affiliations of Middle Eastern Countries (by percentage of population)			
Country	Muslim	Christian	Other
Bahrain	70.3%	14.5%	15.2%
Kuwait	76.7%	17.3%	5.9%
Iran	99.4%	0.3%	0.3%
Lebanon	54.0%	40.5%	5.5%
Qatar	77.5%	8.5%	14.0%

Source: CIA World Factbook, 2014

13. Based on the table, which country is most likely to be affected by multiculturalism?
    a. Bahrain
    b. Kuwait
    c. Iran
    d. Lebanon
    e. Qatar

14. Which of the following best describes the religious composition of Iran?
    a. Iran has experienced significantly more religious syncretism than Bahrain.
    b. Ethnic religions are more popular in Iran compared to neighboring countries.
    c. Iran and Qatar share strong similarities in terms of religious composition.
    d. Christianity likely plays a more influential role in Iran than Kuwait.
    e. The religious composition of Iran is relatively homogenous.

15. Which of the following best describes the process of acculturation?
    a. Acculturation occurs when a minority culture becomes nearly indistinguishable from a majority culture.
    b. Acculturation refers to how a minority culture adapts to a majority culture while still maintaining a unique cultural identity.
    c. Acculturation generally results in entirely new and unique forms of cultural expression.
    d. Acculturation is when multiple distinct cultures have significant impact on a population's cultural practices.
    e. Acculturation is a strategy adopted by minority culture to entirely shield their cultural practices from outside influences.

Answer Explanations

1. A: Ethnocentrism is a perspective on cultural differences, and it's not traditionally a characteristic of cultural landscapes. Thus, Choice *A* is the correct answer. Cultural landscape is an extremely broad concept to describe the relationship between physical environments and human development. Cultural landscapes include forms of economic production, including industrial practices. Therefore, Choice *B* is incorrect. Cultural landscapes also incorporate innumerable cultural aspects, such as land use practices. Therefore, Choice *C* is incorrect. Physical features of the land are a critical aspect of cultural landscapes because they shape the natural environment. Therefore, Choice *D* is incorrect. Sequent occupancy—the cultural legacy of earlier societies that occupied the land—is included in cultural landscapes, so Choice *E* is incorrect.

2. D: The chart depicts a language family. These charts are read in the same hierarchical way as traditional family trees. So, the lines between two languages are the closest connections, representing direct parentage. There's a line connecting Ionic and Epic Greek, which means Epic Greek directly descended from Ionic. Thus, Choice *D* is the correct answer. Choice *A* is incorrect because Greek is directly descended from Koine Greek, not Aeolic. Choice *B* is incorrect because Classical Greek is directly descended from Attic, not Dorian. Choice *C* is incorrect because Greek is directly descended from Koine Greek, not Epic Greek. Although Mycenaean and Aeolic are both descendants of Hellenic, they are not direct descendants of each other, so Choice *E* is incorrect.

3. C: A hearth region of origin is where a cultural trait developed. For this question, each language is a cultural trait. Many of the languages refer to Greece, which is located in the Mediterranean Basin. Thus, Choice *C* is the correct answer. The other answer choices are ancient cultural hearths that are all at least 4,000 years old. While much of the world's culture can be traced back to the ancient cultural hearths through the centuries, a cultural trait's hearth region of origin relates to where it specifically developed. The Fertile Crescent is located in the Middle East, so Choice *A* is incorrect. Indo-Pakistan is located on the Indian subcontinent, so Choice *B* is incorrect. Mexico is located in North America, so Choice *D* is incorrect. Peru is located in South America, so Choice *E* is incorrect.

4. B: Cultural relativism and ethnocentrism are perspectives on cultural differences. Cultural relativism favors comparative descriptions over value judgments, which leads to minimal criticism of cultural practices. Ethnocentrism is the exact opposite, and this perspective often leads to the condemnation of cultural practices it deems harmful. Thus, Choice *B* is the correct answer. Cultural relativism is rarely used to support a claim of cultural superiority, and ethnocentrism isn't directly concerned with a population's ethnic composition. Therefore, Choice *A* is incorrect. Choice *C* is incorrect because cultural relativism has no association with xenophobia (fear of foreign cultures). Choice *D* is incorrect because ethnocentrism is most concerned with its attempts to objectively evaluate culture. Choice *E* is incorrect because it confuses the two perspectives' defining characteristics.

5. A: The map depicts South America in 1776. By this time, European powers had colonized nearly all of South America. Portugal controlled a massive colony in present-day Brazil; France and the Netherlands operated lucrative colonies on the continent's northern coast; and Spain dominated the western half of the continent. The labels on the map refer to these colonies. Thus, Choice *A* is the correct answer. Contagious diffusion is the spread of cultural traits through person-to-person contact, and it's unrelated to European powers' colonization of South America. Therefore, Choice *B* is incorrect. During the 18th century, most European countries adhered to mercantilist economic policies, which rejected free trade. Therefore, Choice *C* is incorrect. Imperialism is very similar to colonialism in terms of its impact at the local level, but European powers didn't adopt imperialist policies until the late 19th century. Therefore, Choice D is incorrect. Some syncretism occurred in South America during this period as European, African, and indigenous cultural practices blended together to create new forms of cultural expression. However, the map isn't depicting syncretic cultural traits, so Choice E is incorrect.

6. E: European powers swiftly conquered South American civilizations and colonized those civilizations' former territories to extract natural resources. Like every other cultural interaction premised on colonization, the colonizers sought to eradicate the colonized people's culture in order to strengthen their own political and social control. Thus, Choice E is the correct answer. Choice A is incorrect because colonizers almost never permit the spread of multiculturalism, viewing it as a threat to their hegemonic rule. Trading with Europeans was not a major concern for most South American civilizations, so Choice B is incorrect. While South American civilizations resisted colonization, this struggle wasn't over the development of syncretic belief systems. In fact, the former inhabitants of South American civilizations readily adopted syncretic belief systems to resist their colonizers. Therefore, Choice C is incorrect. South American civilizations feared European weapons and diseases, not the spread of cultural traits through stimulus diffusion. Therefore, Choice D is incorrect.

7. C: Colonization most frequently results in hierarchical diffusion because colonizers hoped to unilaterally displace local cultural practices and beliefs as quickly as possible. In the Americas, European powers engaged in hierarchical diffusion through government policies and missionary work. Thus, Choice C is the correct answer. Although some indigenous communities did convert to Christianity after personally interacting with belief systems, colonial powers exercised considerable control over the process. Therefore, Choice A is incorrect. Facilitated diffusion isn't a form of cultural diffusion; it's a concept in biology. Therefore, Choice B is incorrect. Relocation diffusion also contributed to the spread of Christianity, but colonial governments still largely controlled the migration patterns. Overall, hierarchical diffusion more accurately describes how most cultural traits spread during colonization. Therefore, Choice D is incorrect. Aside from the development of syncretic belief systems with indigenous and African slave communities, Christianity didn't appreciably change after its introduction in South America, so Choice E is incorrect.

8. A: Contagious diffusion occurs through direct contact between people and/or cultures, resulting in the cultural trait rapidly spreading. The interaction of the local townspeople at the witch trial constitutes direct contact, and the resulting mass hysteria illustrates how a cultural contagion can spread rapidly. Thus, Choice A is the correct answer. Choice B describes relocation diffusion because the cultural trait spreads through immigration. Therefore, Choice B is incorrect. Choice C describes hierarchical diffusion because the feudal lord is imposing a cultural trait on members of a lower socioeconomic class. Therefore, Choice C is incorrect. Choice D describes stimulus diffusion because the fast food chain is altering the menu to facilitate its expansion into a new market. Therefore, Choice D is incorrect. Choice E describes hierarchical diffusion because the cultural trait gradually spreads from the city to suburbs. Therefore, Choice E is incorrect.

9. C: Ethnic religions don't claim to hold universal truths that are applicable to all people, so they expand less aggressively than universalizing religions. As a result, ethnic religions tend to remain most popular in their hearth region of origin, and if they expand at all, it's through relocation diffusion. Hinduism is a classic ethnic religion because it has only spread from its hearth region of origin through relocation diffusion. Thus, Choice C is the correct answer. Buddhism (Choice A), Christianity (Choice B), Islam (Choice D), and Sikhism (Choice E) are all universalizing religions. These four religions assert universal truths, and they have all spread through both relocation diffusion and expansion diffusion. Therefore, Choice A, Choice B, Choice D, and Choice E are incorrect.

10. B: The seven ancient cultural hearths had such a lasting legacy because they all successfully domesticated plants and animals earlier than other societies. Large-scale agriculture and animal husbandry produced a food surplus, facilitating the development of complex economic systems and increasing the pace of cultural interactions. Thus, Choice *B* is the correct answer. The development of the ancient cultural hearths predates industrialization by more than 4,000 years, so Choice *A* is incorrect. Islam and Christianity developed in the Fertile Crescent, and Buddhism and Sikhism developed in Indo-Pakistan before spreading to East India. However, the other four hearths didn't birth a universalizing religion, so Choice *C* is incorrect. Likewise, the Indo-European language family is one of the largest and most influential language families in human history, but it was not shared by all the ancient cultural hearths. China, Ethiopia, Mexico, and Peru all developed their own unique ancient language families, so Choice *D* is incorrect. The ancient cultural hearths were pre-industrial societies, so they experienced high fertility and mortality rates. Therefore, they didn't face issues due to aging populations, so Choice *E* is incorrect.

11. D: Culture can be transmitted in nearly endless ways, ranging from governmental policies to entertainment consumption. Furthermore, culture can be transmitted intentionally or spontaneously. For example, powerful institutions can sometimes unilaterally shift the culture to achieve a goal, but other times cultural change is a natural byproduct of social interactions that spirals in an unforeseen direction. Thus, Choice *D* is the correct answer. Culture is not always transmitted through hierarchical relationships. For example, relocation diffusion and contagious diffusion can occur outside of hierarchical relationships, so Choice *A* is incorrect. Religion, economic activities, and government policies play a powerful role in cultural development, but culture can be transmitted in other important ways, such as through social interactions and digital networks. Therefore, Choice *B* is incorrect. Choice *C* is a true statement, but it does not describe how culture is transmitted across society, so it's incorrect. Choice *E* is incorrect because there are many functional definitions of culture, and geographers regularly trace the history of cultural traits back to the ancient cultural hearths.

12. E: Buddhism developed on the Indian subcontinent, so Choice *A* is incorrect. Christianity developed in Judea, so Choice *B* is incorrect. Hinduism also developed on the Indian subcontinent, so Choice *C* is incorrect. Islam developed in the Middle East, so Choice *D* is incorrect. Sikhism is another world religion that developed on the Indian subcontinent, which is located in South Asia. Thus, Choice *E* is the correct answer.

13. D: Multiculturalism develops when multiple distinct cultures in a single society simultaneously influence the society's cultural development. Of the five countries listed in the table, Lebanon seems like the outlier. The other four countries have a single religion account for more than 70% of total religious followers. In contrast, Islam only accounts for 54% of Lebanese religious followers, and 40.5% of the population practices Christianity. With two sizable and distinct religious faiths, Lebanon is the most likely to be affected by multiculturalism. Thus, Choice *D* is the correct answer. Based on the table, there seems to be considerable religious diversity in Bahrain (Choice *A*), Kuwait (Choice *B*), and Qatar (Choice *E*), and they all could be influenced by multiculturalism. However, Lebanon is the most definitely multicultural, so Choices *A*, *B*, and *E* are incorrect. Iran is overwhelmingly a Muslim country, so Choice *C* is incorrect.

14. E: According to the table, 99.4% of Iran's religious followers adhere to Islam. This means Iran's religious composition is homogeneous, meaning the country's religious followers are alike in terms of religious affiliation. Thus, Choice *E* is the correct answer. Choice *A* is incorrect because the table doesn't provide information about religious syncretism, and, in any event, a blending of religious beliefs would be more likely to occur in Bahrain than Iran due to Bahrain's greater religious diversity. Islam is a universalizing religion, and nearly all Iranians are Muslim. Therefore, Choice *B* is incorrect. Qatar has

31

significantly more religious diversity than Iran, so Choice *C* is incorrect. Christianity accounts for 0.3% and 17.3% of total religious followers in Iran and Kuwait, respectively, so Choice *D* is incorrect.

15. B: Acculturation occurs when the influence of a majority culture alters a minority culture's beliefs or practices, but the minority culture continues to be identifiable as a unique and distinct cultural entity. This differs from assimilation, which leads to the minority culture strongly resembling the majority culture. Thus, Choice *B* is the correct answer. Choice *A* is incorrect because it describes assimilation more than acculturation. Choice *C* is incorrect because it states the consequence of syncretism. Choice *D* is incorrect because it summarizes multiculturalism. Choice *E* is incorrect because acculturation doesn't entirely shield the minority culture from the majority culture. Although the minority culture survives acculturation largely intact, interaction with majority culture does result in some changes.

Political Patterns and Processes

Introduction to Political Geography

Several types of political entities appear on world political maps. **Nations** are distinct communities with numerous shared cultural characteristics, including ethnicity, history, land, language, and religion. **States** are a community of people living under a common system of government. In general, states seek to maximize their independence by establishing sovereignty, meaning a government's ability to exercise unilateral and supreme authority over its territories. In the present day, independent states serve as the foundation of world political maps because they have the authority and power to delineate political boundaries.

The French Revolution (1789–1799) spurred the development of a nation-state, which aligned cultural and political boundaries. As such, **nation-states** have a distinct cultural community and common system of government. **Multinational states** enjoy sovereign control over multiple nations. Examples of multinational states on the contemporary world political map include Afghanistan, Canada, India, Russia, and the United States. **Supranational states** are a new type of multinational state in which the member states cede some degree of sovereignty to an intergovernmental system. The European Union (EU) is the quintessential example of a supranational state.

Multistate nations are a community of people with shared cultural characteristics who live in several different states. For example, the Kurds are a distinct cultural community with a significant presence in Iran, Iraq, Turkey, and Syria. Some multistate nations, including the Kurds, are **stateless nations**, which refer to distinct cultural communities that aren't the majority population in any nation-state. Other contemporary examples of stateless nations include the Uyghur people in China, the Yoruba and Igbo peoples in Nigeria, and the Québécois people in Canada.

At times, nation-states include autonomous and semiautonomous regions. Nation-state governments typically retain sovereignty over autonomous and semiautonomous regions, but they grant these regions limited freedoms and political independence. In most cases, nation-state governments tolerate the establishment of these autonomous regions because they are difficult to govern due to geographic challenges, cultural reasons, and/or political pressure. The distinction between autonomous and semiautonomous regions is subjective and depends on a region's degree of self-government. Contemporary examples of these regions include American Indian reservations, Iraqi Kurdistan, and Somaliland. Although the delegation of limited political freedom to autonomous regions can promote peaceful relations, it can also lead to conflict. For example, since the Iraqi government recognized the autonomy of Iraqi Kurdistan in 2005, the two political entities have engaged in a prolonged and heated conflict over political authority, territorial claims, and control over natural resources.

Political Processes

Sovereignty, Nation-States, and Self-Determination

Contemporary political geography has been shaped by historical processes, such as the development of nation-states, sovereignty, and self-determination.

All three of these critical concepts have a common foundation in the Treaty of Westphalia (1648), which sought to establish peace after the Thirty Years' War. The **Treaty of Westphalia** recognized the sovereignty of princes in the Holy Roman Empire, and princes were allowed to independently determine their states' religion. The concept of a nation-state naturally developed out of these changes because the princes served as sovereign rulers over distinct communities.

The French Revolution redefined the concept of a nation-state by implementing the political model of popular sovereignty. Under this political model, citizens functioned as the source of political authority. Furthermore, as the revolutionaries rebuilt France, they stoked nationalism by increasing civic participation to unify the country. Following Napoleon's conquest of mainland Europe, the French Revolution's ideas about nationalism and sovereignty spread across the continent.

After World War II, the newly created United Nations (UN) legally endorsed states' right to self-determination, which includes citizens' right to choose how they're governed. So, for the first time in modern history, the concepts of nation-states, sovereignty, and self-determination theoretically applied everywhere in the world. Since the end of World War II, sovereign nation-states have functioned as the basic building blocks in political geography.

Colonialism, Imperialism, Independence Movements, and Devolution

Historical processes have similarly influenced contemporary political boundaries. European colonialism and imperialism left a lasting impact on the contemporary political map. When independence movements secured the right to self-government, the resulting states retained their former colonial borders. This process proved problematic because the colonizers disregarded local culture and history when carving up the land. As a result, some of the newly established states experienced devolution due to the presence of antagonistic cultural groups. For example, British India underwent a series of partitions that resulted in the establishment of modern-day India, Pakistan, and Bangladesh.

Two relatively recent large-scale devolutions triggered by nationalist independence movements have resulted in major changes to the contemporary political map. First, the Soviet Union's dissolution in the late 1980s led to the creation of fifteen new nation-states—Armenia, Azerbaijan, Belarus, Estonia, Georgia, Kazakhstan, Kyrgyzstan, Latvia, Lithuania, Moldova, Russia, Tajikistan, Turkmenistan, Ukraine, and Uzbekistan. Second, nationalist independence movements caused the breakup of Yugoslavia during the early 1990s, and it was ultimately succeeded by Bosnia and Herzegovina, Croatia, Kosovo, Montenegro, North Macedonia, Serbia, and Slovenia.

Political Power and Territoriality

Geographers use political power to describe efforts to control land, accumulate resources, and influence the behavior of individuals and groups. Political entities can exercise political power through the enforcement of laws, cultural influence, diplomacy, military force, and economic coercion. Additionally, political power is often exercised to increase territorially, meaning people's shared connections to the land based on cultural, economic, and historical factors.

Political Power

Political entities regularly exercise political power in a geographic context to implement neocolonial policies, dominate shatterbelts, and seize choke points.

European states adopted **neocolonialism** in the aftermath of decolonization during the Cold War. Rather than direct governance, European states leveraged existing commercial relationships in their former colonies to gain uninterrupted access to natural resources and cheap labor markets. Supporters of free trade reject the label of neocolonialism and highlight multinational corporations' role in creating higher-

paying jobs in the developing world. In response, critics point to how neocolonialism has led to human rights abuses and environmental destruction.

Shatterbelts are closely related to neocolonialism because they are geographic areas without a functional government, making them the ideal location for world powers to extend their political and economic influence. During the Cold War, the United States and Soviet Union competed for shatterbelts in South America, Africa, the Middle East, Eastern Europe, and Southeast Asia. In the present day, the Middle East is the most active shatterbelt. For example, the United States, Russia, Iran, and Turkey have all intervened in the Syrian Civil War to support regional allies, maintain border security, and secure interests in a proposed oil pipeline to Europe.

Choke points are narrow geographic areas, such as valleys and straits, that restrict military operations and/or economic activity. As a result, world powers battle for choke points to maximize their geographic dominance over the surrounding land. One of the most valuable contemporary choke points is the Strait of Hormuz on the Persian Gulf, located between Oman and Iran. Approximately 33 percent of the world's natural gas and 25 percent of the global oil supply is shipped through the Strait of Hormuz. As a result, control over the Strait of Hormuz is a major source of tension between the United States and Iran.

Territoriality

Political entities value **territoriality** because it increases citizens' commitment to and investment in the state's political and economic system. Throughout modern history, political leaders have emphasized people's connections to land because it legitimizes and unifies nation-states. The most common method of emphasizing those connections is the promotion of nationalism. Contemporary political entities increase nationalism by elevating symbols of national pride, encouraging citizens to fulfill civic duties, and rejecting the economic and cultural effects of globalization.

Defining Political Boundaries

Geographers use a variety of **political boundaries** when analyzing political entities. Although **relic political boundaries** are no longer active, they have a lasting legacy due to their cultural or geographic impact. For example, the Great Wall of China hasn't had a functional purpose since the Ming Dynasty (1368–1644), but it shaped the creation of the states that later developed into modern-day China. **Superimposed boundaries** are forced on a people, typically with little to no regard for cultural differences. European colonialism is responsible for the vast numbers of superimposed boundaries, especially in Africa and the Middle East. **Subsequent political boundaries**, such as the border between the United States and Canada, evolve alongside the development of a nation-state. **Antecedent political boundaries** existed prior to the development of nation-states, such as how the Himalayan Mountains separate China from India. **Geometric political boundaries** are relatively straight lines or arcs that are drawn on a map without any regard for geographic or cultural characteristics, such as the border between North Korea and South Korea at the thirty-eighth parallel. **Consequent boundaries** separate geographic areas based on cultural differences, including religion, language, and ethnicity. For example, the border between India and Pakistan can be classified as a consequent boundary.

Function of Political Boundaries

Political entities delimit and demarcate boundaries to define the maximum extent of their sovereign territory. In effect, political boundaries create areas in which the government can exercise political authority, as expressed through the promulgation and enforcement of laws. There are two types of political boundaries—international and internal.

International boundaries serve as a state's outer boundaries. For example, a shared border between two states is an international boundary. Unsurprisingly, international boundaries are often hotly contested because states simultaneously seek to protect their sovereignty while also expanding their political and economic influence. As a result, international borders are usually highly regulated and feature extensive checkpoints. International treaties have established the vast majority of international boundaries, and the Charter of the UN prohibits the violation of a state's territorial integrity to reduce border conflicts. Unlike international boundaries, **internal boundaries** don't demarcate the maximum extent of a state's sovereignty. Instead, internal boundaries facilitate the government's ability to administer electoral systems, deliver government services, and maintain economic oversight. Examples of internal boundaries include state lines, county lines, townships and ranges, municipal zones, and voting districts.

Contemporary Political Boundaries

Contemporary political boundaries tend to align with national, cultural, and economic characteristics. In nation-states, the people living within the borders share a distinct national identity. Likewise, in some multinational states, internal boundaries generally reflect the states' cultural and national divisions. Furthermore, internal political boundaries are often set based on the dominant type of economic production within a given geographic area. **Economic-based political boundaries** are particularly prevalent when production is predicated on an industry's proximity to natural resources, such as fossil fuels, timber, and mineral deposits.

Other types of political boundaries are the by-product of military conflict and foreign interventions. To prevent a recurrence of hostilities, peace treaties sometimes establish **demilitarized zones** in border regions to serve as buffer zones. For example, the Korean Demilitarized Zone runs alongside the thirty-eighth parallel on the Korean Peninsula, and it was created after the Korean War (1950–1953) to deter a large-scale invasion. Although demilitarized zones prohibit military activities within the designated geographic area, states often prevent people from crossing the zone and heavily fortify their side of the border. **Unilateral foreign interventions** also have a long history of shaping political boundaries, dating back to European colonization in the sixteenth century. For example, European powers met at the Berlin Conference of 1884–1885 to jointly set colonial boundaries during the Scramble for Africa (1881–1914), and those boundaries were incorporated into African states after they gained independence.

Land and Maritime Boundaries

International agreements and political boundaries have a profound effect on national and regional identity. When international agreements create more fluid political boundaries, regional identity can be strengthened. For example, the EU reinvigorated the notion of a European identity by abolishing internal border controls to facilitate the free movement of people between member states. International agreements, such as the North American Free Trade Agreement, Mercosur (South American trading bloc), and Association of Southeast Asian Nations (ASEAN), can also result in more internal and international commercial interactions by removing barriers to trade. On the other hand, nationalist governments frequently tighten border controls and reject free-trade agreements to protect national identity from the effects of globalization. Militarized land boundaries can also reduce commercial interactions and trigger border conflicts over resources. At times, international agreements, such as the implementation of the Antarctic Treaty System in 1961 to preserve the wilderness for

scientific research, have been signed to prevent states from competing over natural resources and expanding their territorial borders.

Disputes over maritime boundaries can also similarly limit commerce and/or trigger international disputes. For example, the United States and Southeast Asian states have challenged Chinese maritime claims in the South China Sea, especially China's militarization of man-made islands. Likewise, disputes over maritime resources, such as fisheries and oil deposits, have disrupted international relations and undermined commercial relationships. In many circumstances, maritime agreements are difficult to enforce because the conflicts occur in distant and isolated areas.

United Nations Convention on the Law of the Sea (UNCLOS)

The **United Nations Convention on the Law of the Sea (UNCLOS)** establishes states' rights and responsibilities in international waters. This widely supported international agreement has been in effect since 1992, and it has three critical provisions. First, UNCLOS codified the freedom of the sea as international law, effectively prohibiting states from claiming sovereignty over international waters. Second, UNCLOS allowed states to claim sovereignty over territorial seas with a maximum range of up to 12 nautical miles from their coasts. However, foreign military and civilian ships enjoy the right of innocent passage through territorial seas, though such actions can trigger diplomatic conflicts. Third, UNCLOS provided states with EEZs that extend up to 200 nautical miles from their coasts. EEZs grant states with special rights and privileges to conduct commercial activities, including fishing, energy production, and drilling.

Internal Boundaries

International and Internal Boundaries

Political entities establish internal boundaries to increase the efficiency of administering government services and/or alter how citizens are represented in the government. In terms of administering government services, central governments rely on internal boundaries to determine the extent of political authority and resources that must be delegated at the local level.

To determine how people are represented in republican systems of governments, political entities use internal boundaries to create voting districts. Within each voting district, there are numerous polling areas where people vote in national and subnational elections. Depending on the system of government, control over voting districts can be vested in the central government, subnational governments, or both in accordance with some power-sharing scheme. Voting districts usually contain a uniform number of people, and most governments regularly hold a census to determine population changes. When voting districts experience population changes, governments conduct redistricting to alter their size. Redistricting can be controversial when a powerful political party redraws the internal boundaries to gain a partisan advantage. This type of manipulative redistricting is referred to as **gerrymandering**. A common form of gerrymandering involves spreading the opposing political party's voters across multiple districts to prevent them from forming a majority.

Forms of Governance

Federal and Unitary States

Contemporary states are either organized as federal or unitary states. **Federal states** share political power between the central government and subnational units of government. Consequently, the political administration of federal states typically involves a complex series of checks and balances. Some political powers are specifically reserved for the central government and subnational units of government, whereas other powers are mutually shared. Political power sharing creates considerable flexibility, facilitating the governance of vast territories. On the other hand, the central government under a federal system must strike a balance between the subnational governmental units' disparate goals and values. These differences can sometimes create a logjam that grinds the entire system of government to a halt. Examples of contemporary federal states include Belgium, Canada, Germany, India, Russia, and the United States.

Unitary states consolidate power in a central government. Although unitary states often include subnational units of government, the central government is the source of their political power. As a result, unitary states' central governments can unilaterally alter the scope of their subnational units' authority and political power. For example, a unitary state's central government could invalidate a subnational unit's law. Some unitary states, such as Chile, Finland, France, South Africa, and South Korea, have republican systems of government. At the same time, unitary states' all-powerful central governments can lend themselves to autocratic rule. Examples of autocratic unitary states include China, Egypt, North Korea, and Saudi Arabia. In general, unitary states can implement new policies more efficiently than federal states, especially policies that are a dramatic departure from earlier policies. However, unitary states are generally less responsive to localized political movements, particularly when those movements challenge the central government.

How Federal and Unitary States Affect Spatial Organization

Federal and unitary states both have a significant impact on spatial organization. Because federal states have relatively more independent subnational units of government, those areas tend to have a more developed capital city and complex system of local government. In contrast, unitary states can create or abolish subnational units at will, so the spatial organization of local government is much more fluid. In addition, political power and wealth is more likely to flow toward the central government's seat of power. Unitary states' central governments also typically provide more direction in regard to natural resource consumption and the development of national supply chains, so industries are more interdependent on a national level. Although industries in federal states are also interdependent, regional economic factors tend to have a disproportionately greater influence on local economic development when compared to unitary states.

Defining Devolutionary Factors

Devolution of States

Devolution refers to central governments transferring political power to subnational units of government, such as regions, states, provinces, counties, and municipalities. Although devolution is relatively more common in federal states, it can also occur in unitary states. However, unitary states' central governments can unilaterally withdraw the delegation of political power. When devolution fails to adequately resolve underlying tensions between the central government and its subnational governments, the weaker central government can lose its legitimacy, triggering the dissolution of the state.

Five factors can contribute to the devolution of states. First, physical geography can cause devolution when the central government cannot effectively and efficiently oversee its subnational governments. Second, the central government might willingly grant or be forced to provide subnational governments with more autonomy to curb support for ethnic separatist movements. Third, ethnic cleansing and terrorism can result in devolution when the central government loses the ability to maintain law and order within its territories. Fourth, economic and social problems can lead to devolution when the

central government becomes destabilized. Fifth, irredentism refers to states' claims over land they consider part of their historic territory, and it can force devolution when foreign states successfully annex the disputed land.

Challenges to Sovereignty

State sovereignty faces a diverse array of political, economic, cultural, and technological challenges. Political challenges to state sovereignty typically arise when the central government suffers from destabilizing factors, including corruption and separatist movements. Economic challenges to state sovereignty typically relate to growth rates, regional development, and income inequality. Cultural challenges over the states' values and social systems can be highly divisive, and they're most prominent in multinational states. Finally, technological challenges most commonly arise through the dissemination of information and enhanced potential for communication.

When Devolution Occurs

Devolution refers to central governments ceding some degree of sovereignty to subnational units of government. Overwhelmingly, central governments are coerced into devolution to relieve political pressure as challenges mount against their sovereignty. There are three common methods of devolution.

First, devolution can occur through a greater delegation of power to subnational units of government. After a series of coups and civil wars, Nigeria implemented a federal system of government in the early 1970s, and it has since created dozens of new states. Similarly, when cultural conflicts between the Flanders and Wallonia regions critically destabilized Belgium's central government in the 1960s, it transitioned from a unitary to a federal state. During the early 1990s, Canada created the Nunavut territory to settle land claims with the Inuit peoples and expedite the development of Canada's most northern territories.

Second, central governments can implement devolution through the establishment of autonomous regions. For example, Spain has seventeen autonomous communities and two autonomous cities. The Spanish central government originally granted autonomy under the Constitution of 1978 to prevent the state from breaking up as it enacted democratic reforms. However, some regions have demanded even greater levels of autonomy, such as Catalonia's ongoing attempts to secede from Spain.

Third, devolution can be the end result of civil wars, separatist movements, international agreements, and/or state disintegration. The state of Eritrea formed after separatists wore out Ethiopian forces during a protracted civil war (1961–1991). Similarly, South Sudan gained independence in 2011 after separatists fought two lengthy civil wars against Sudan (1955–1972; 1983–2005). The UN intervened in East Timor to end Indonesia's brutal occupation (1975–1999), and East Timor secured its long-awaited independence by international agreement in 2001. Combined with a prolonged economic downturn, Eastern European nationalist movements triggered the disintegration of the Soviet Union in the late 1980s.

Advances in Communication Technologies

Communication technologies have spurred devolution, democratization, and supranationalism. Western radio broadcasts and television programs galvanized Eastern European nationalist movements in their resistance to Soviet domination. Likewise, televised interviews with investigative journalists played a critical role in forcing the United States to end its support for Indonesia, especially after Indonesian forces massacred more than a thousand East Timorese voters in 1999. Social media connected and amplified grassroots democratization movements across the Middle East during the Arab Spring (2010–2012). Digital communications have enabled the development and management of supranational organizations, including the North American Free Trade Agreement and EU.

Transnational and Environmental Challenges

Supranationalism concerns international economic, political, and military cooperation. States most frequently pursue supranationalism through economies of scale, free-trade agreements, military alliances, and international efforts to tackle transnational and environmental issues. Economies of scale result in costs decreasing as production increases. States often encourage the formation of multinational corporations to stimulate higher levels of production. Free-trade agreements remove barriers to trade, such as tariffs and subsidies for domestic industries. Free trade has increased exponentially since the end of the Cold War, resulting in the creation of a more integrated global market. Military alliances typically include provisions on common defense, transfers of sensitive technologies, and the sharing of intelligence.

Transnational issues include refugee crises, terrorism, organized criminal networks, human trafficking, and cybercrime. In response to these issues, states have formed joint task forces to prevent and prosecute crimes that cross national borders. Likewise, states often allocate resources and sign international agreements to address shared environmental challenges, such as climate change and marine pollution.

Supranational Organizations

Member states delegate some degree of sovereignty to supranational organizations for the purpose of increasing international cooperation on specifically designated issues. As such, states' membership in supranational organizations can restrict or force states to take some economic or political actions when doing so would violate the terms of the underlying international agreement. Free-trade blocs, such as those established by the EU and ASEAN, limit members' ability to place tariffs on certain goods and services. Similarly, the Arctic Council prevents members from taking certain actions that would threaten the environment, such as drilling in sensitive geographic areas. Military alliances, such as the NATO, generally force the alliance to participate in military actions when a member is attacked. In addition, many supranational organizations, including the UN and AU, can condemn, sanction, and intervene against members that violate its resolutions.

Consequences of Centrifugal and Centripetal Forces

The American geographer Richard Hartshorne developed a theory of centrifugal and centripetal forces to explain integration at the state scale. Centrifugal forces exacerbate divisions. Examples of **centrifugal forces** include income inequality, government corruption, separatist movements, and antagonistic cultural elements. In contrast, **centripetal forces** are factors that increase integration over territory, such as economic prosperity, strong infrastructure networks, united national identity, and cohesive culture. When centripetal forces overpower the centrifugal forces, the state is more likely to secure cultural, economic, political, and social integration. In the inverse situation, centrifugal forces have the potential to sow dysfunction and undermine the state's legitimacy.

Centrifugal Forces

Centrifugal forces have an incredibly destructive impact on states. Income inequality, especially at the regional level, can lead to uneven development. If the working class and regions feel left behind economically, they could be incentivized to seek regime change or greater autonomy. Similarly, ethnic nationalist movements can bolster popular opposition to the state's claims of sovereignty and lend

support to independence movements. For example, during the early 1990s, ethnic nationalist movements incited a series of brutal civil wars in the Balkans that led to the breakup of Yugoslavia. Religion can similarly fuel separatist movements. During the Troubles (1966–1998), the overwhelmingly Catholic Irish republicans leveraged historical antagonism toward British Anglicanism to gain popular support for Northern Ireland's secession from the United Kingdom. Likewise, stateless nations can present a challenge to sovereignty, such as Kurds' ongoing insurrection against the Turkish government. Overall, if states fail to effectively quell centrifugal forces, they risk becoming failed states. Common characteristics of failed states include the collapse of political authority, inability to conduct, loss of territorial integrity, and loss of basic state functions.

Centripetal Forces

Centripetal forces can have both positive and negative impacts on the development of states. State investment in infrastructure networks, such as national freeways and public transportation systems, can integrate regional economies and facilitate travel across the state. Greater cultural cohesion can reduce societal tensions, so states often seek to adopt policies that embrace multiculturalism. Nationalism can also bolster cultural cohesion by rejecting globalization and influence in artistic movements, entertainment, music, and other cultural characteristics. However, nationalism can sometimes evolve into ethnonationalism when it is connected to the state's dominant ethnicity. Ethnonationalism can incentivize states to pass harsh immigration policies and persecute minority groups, so it can transform into a centrifugal force when minority groups pursue autonomy to escape state persecution.

Practice Questions

Questions 1 and 2 refer to the graph below.

Foreign Trade of the United Kingdom

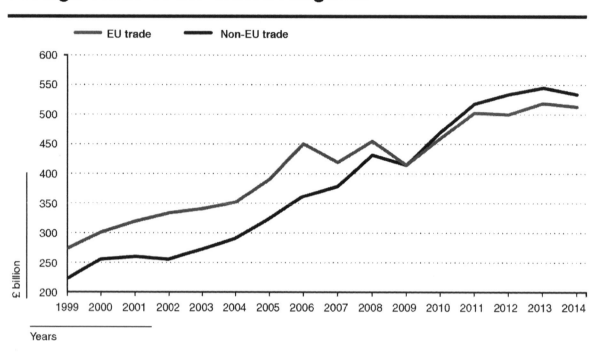

1. Which of the following best explains the trends expressed on the graph?
   a. The United Kingdom has free-trade agreements with nearly every state in the world.
   b. The United Kingdom's trade with the European Union (EU) matches or exceeds its trade with the rest of the world because the EU is a free-trade bloc.
   c. The United Kingdom has historically rejected supranationalism in all forms, which is why it overwhelmingly trades with neighboring states.
   d. The United Kingdom primarily engages in trade to address supranational challenges.
   e. The United Kingdom is a unitary state, so it relies on international trade to counteract deficiencies in regional economic production.

2. Based on the trends expressed on the graph, which of the following will most likely occur when the United Kingdom completes its withdrawal from the European Union?
   a. The United Kingdom will likely import significantly more goods from European Union (EU) member states.
   b. The United Kingdom will likely stop pursuing bilateral free-trade agreements.
   c. The United Kingdom will likely trade more with the rest of the world than with the EU.
   d. The United Kingdom will likely cede some degree of sovereignty over economic decisions to another supranational organization.
   e. The United Kingdom will likely seek to attract more foreign investment from EU member states.

3. Which of the following provides the correct definition for multinational states?
    a. Multinational states contain multiple nation-states and transcend national boundaries.
    b. Multinational states have both a distinct cultural community and common system of government.
    c. Multinational states contain distinct cultural communities that aren't the majority population in any other nation-state.
    d. Multinational states have sovereign control over multiple distinct communities of people.
    e. Multinational states feature autonomous regions to better integrate diverse cultural communities.

Question 4 refers to the table below.

Internet Rates in Bahrain	
Year	**Rate (% population)**
2005	21
2006	28
2007	33
2008	52
2009	53
2010	55
2011	77
2012	88
2013	90

Source: World Bank Group (2019)

4. The trend depicted in the graph most likely influenced which of the following historical events?
    a. Bahraini activists held large-scale protests to call for democratization during the Arab Spring in 2011.
    b. The Bahraini government successfully negotiated a bilateral free-trade agreement with the United States in 2006.
    c. Bahraini military forces provided Saudi Arabia with military, logistical, and technological support to bomb Yemeni rebels in 2015.
    d. Illegal foreign workers applied for amnesty granted by the Bahraini government in 2007.
    e. Bahrain became the first Arab state to appoint a Jewish ambassador in 2008.

5. Which of the following most accurately summarizes European states' historic influence on African political boundaries?
    a. African states sought the expertise of European states when deciding where to place political boundaries.
    b. European states carefully crafted African political boundaries to reflect local populations' cultural and historical differences.
    c. European colonizers rejected the concept of political boundaries, and African states have maintained the tradition of having open borders.
    d. European colonialism and imperialism resulted in African states adopting geometric political boundaries.
    e. Newly independent African states generally accepted European colonies' political boundaries.

Questions 6–8 refer to the map below.

Overlapping Claims in the South China Sea

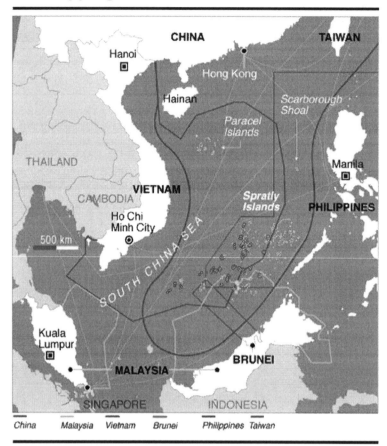

6. Based on the map, which of the following geographic areas likely involves the most complex series of competing sovereign claims?
    a. Hainan
    b. Kuala Lumpur
    c. Paracel Islands
    d. Scarborough Shoal
    e. Spratly Islands

7. Which of the following international agreements is the most directly relevant for evaluating the claims expressed on the map?
    a. Association of Southeast Asian Nations (ASEAN)
    b. Convention on Facilitation of International Maritime Traffic (FAL Convention)
    c. International Convention for the Safety of Life at Sea (SOLAS)
    d. International Maritime Organization (IMO)
    e. United Nations Convention on the Law of the Sea (UNCLOS)

8. Which of the following provides the primary benefit of exclusive economic zones (EEZs)?
   a. States may exploit maritime resources for economic gain and deny foreign ships the right to innocent passage.
   b. States enjoy special economic rights and privileges within 200 nautical miles of their coasts.
   c. States enjoy sovereign control over waterways within 12 nautical miles of their coasts.
   d. States can build militarized structures, such as man-made islands, to protect maritime-based economic production.
   e. States may exercise the right to change maritime political boundaries through bilateral international agreements.

9. Which of the following is NOT currently a unitary state?
   a. Belgium
   b. China
   c. Egypt
   d. France
   e. Saudi Arabia

Question 10 refers to the photograph below.

Kutupalong Refugee Camp in Bangladesh (2017)

Source: John Owens, Voice of America

10. Which of the following most likely contributed to the situation depicted in the photograph?
     a. Centrifugal forces
     b. Centripetal forces
     c. Devolution
     d. Technological challenges
     e. Shatterbelts

11. Which of the following best describes the relationship between sovereignty and territoriality?
     a. Sovereignty is held by central governments, whereas subnational units of government enjoy rights to territoriality.
     b. Territoriality refers to control over territory, whereas sovereignty is related to political organization.
     c. Political entities leverage territoriality to protect their sovereignty.
     d. Territoriality is generally more valuable to political entities than sovereignty.
     e. Sovereignty is entirely incompatible with territoriality.

Questions 12 and 13 refer to the map below.

European NATO members (2019)

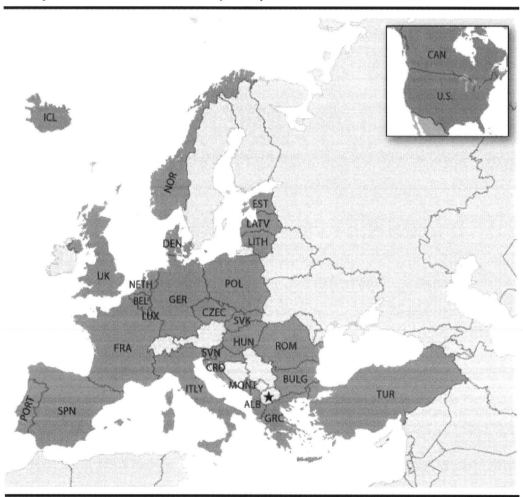

12. The map depicts which of the following types of organizations?
    a. Free-trade organization
    b. International financial organization
    c. Joint task force for transnational challenges
    d. Military alliance
    e. Supranational political union

13. Which of the following best explains why the members have joined this organization?
    a. The organization increases members' sovereignty by protecting their territorial integrity.
    b. The organization offers a framework for widespread international cooperation in economic, military, and political matters.
    c. The organization provides for the common defense of members and facilitates the transfer of sensitive technologies.
    d. The organization helps members secure greater levels of foreign direct investment.
    e. The organization optimizes how members approach transnational challenges, such as terrorism and organized crime.

14. Which of the following most accurately describes how ethnic separatist movements can lead to devolution?
    a. Ethnic separatist movements provide the foundation for subnational units of government.
    b. Ethnic separatist movements function as centripetal forces at the state scale.
    c. Ethnic separatist movements rally international support to expedite state disintegration.
    d. Ethnic separatist movements can incite civil wars and/or secure more autonomy.
    e. Ethnic separatist movements advocate for unitary states to incorporate more federalism.

Question 15 refers to the diagram below.

Redistricting

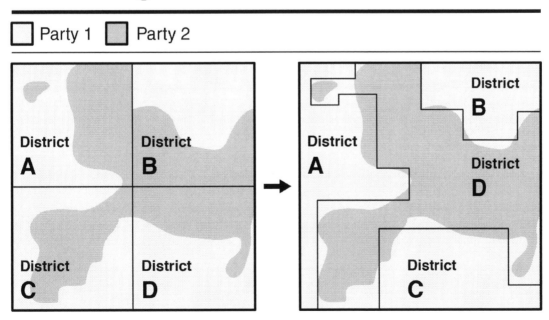

15. The diagram illustrates which of the following manipulative redistricting practices?
    a. Contiguity
    b. Gerrymandering
    c. Partisan fairness
    d. Proportional representation
    e. Reapportionment

Answer Explanations

1. B: The graph expresses the United Kingdom's trade with the European Union (EU) in comparison to the rest of the world. Depending on the year, the United Kingdom's trade with the EU either exceeds or nearly matches its trade with the rest of the world. This disproportionate emphasis on European trade was the direct product of the United Kingdom's membership in the EU's free-trade bloc. As a result, the United Kingdom can import European goods and export its products to Europe at cheaper costs due to the elimination of trade barriers within the bloc. Thus, Choice *B* is the correct answer. The United Kingdom doesn't have free-trade agreements with every state, which is why it prefers to trade with certain partners. So, Choice *A* is incorrect. Given the United Kingdom's former membership in the EU and current membership in the North Atlantic Treaty Organization (NATO), it's not accurate to say the country historically rejects supranationalism. As such, Choice *C* is incorrect. Like most states, the United Kingdom primarily trades to stimulate economic growth, so Choice *D* is incorrect. Although the United Kingdom is a unitary state, it doesn't engage in trade for explicitly regional purposes. Therefore, Choice *E* is incorrect.

2. C: The graph indicates that the United Kingdom's trade with the European Union (EU) accounts for a disproportionate amount of its total trade. So, when the United Kingdom finally completes its long-awaited withdrawal from the EU, it will lose many of the benefits of membership, including unfettered access to the trade bloc. This will naturally result in less trade with the EU. Consequently, based on the trend expressed on the graph, the United Kingdom's trade with the rest of the world will almost certainly exceed its trade with the EU. Thus, Choice *C* is the correct answer. For the reasons described above, the United Kingdom will import fewer European goods in the near future. So, Choice *A* is incorrect. Although public opinion in the United Kingdom has turned against the EU, it will still need other bilateral free-trade agreements to maintain current levels of production. Therefore, Choice *B* is incorrect. Choice *D* is incorrect because the United Kingdom withdrew from the EU to recover the sovereignty it had ceded to supranationalism. There's no indication in the graph or anywhere else that the United Kingdom will be eager to do so again. The United Kingdom will lose a significant amount of European foreign investment when it fully withdraws from the EU, so Choice *E* is incorrect.

3. D: As implied in the name, multinational states contain multiple nations within their borders. When used in this context, the concept of nations is referring to distinct communities of people that are bound by shared characteristics, such as language, religion, and connections to the land. Thus, Choice *D* is the correct answer. Choice *A* is incorrect because multinational states contain multiple nations, not nation-states. Choice *B* is incorrect because it states the definition of a nation-state. Choice *C* is incorrect because it describes a characteristic of stateless nations. Choice *E* is incorrect because the incorporation of autonomous regions is only a possibility and not a defining characteristic.

4. A: The Arab Spring featured greater calls for democracy across the Middle East during the early 2010s. This political movement was especially noteworthy because it was the first time activists used social media to build grassroots support and coordinate large-scale protests. If Bahrainis' access to the Internet didn't increase in the run-up to the Arab Spring, the country's autocratic government would have had a much easier time suppressing dissent. Thus, Choice *A* is the correct answer. All of the other answer choices accurately describe historical events, but increased Internet access among the broader public wasn't a major cause of those events. Although increased Internet access helped modernize the Bahraini economy, it wasn't directly related to the country's trade deal with the United States. So, Choice *B* is incorrect. Similarly, greater public access to the Internet didn't facilitate Bahrain's military using sophisticated military technologies, so Choice *C* is incorrect. The Bahraini government's decision to grant workers with amnesty is completely unrelated to Internet access, and therefore, Choice *D* is incorrect. Choice *E* is incorrect because public usage of the Internet wouldn't influence the appointment of an ambassador in an autocratic state.

5. E: European powers colonized nearly the entire African continent during a period known as the Scramble for Africa (1881–1914). When African states gained independence in the aftermath of World War II, they generally retained the colonial boundaries. Thus, Choice *E* is the correct answer. Choice *A* is incorrect because European states didn't consult with African groups or leaders as they unilaterally carved up the continent. Choice *B* is incorrect because European powers infamously didn't consider the consequences of placing political boundaries across historic tribal lands. Choice *C* is incorrect on all accounts. European powers established political boundaries to protect their colonies, and they met at the Berlin Conference (1884–1885) to coordinate the drawing of those boundaries. In addition, no functional African state has ever had open borders. Choice *D* is incorrect because the colonial borders are classified as subsequent political boundaries.

6. E: The Spratly Islands are one of the most hotly disputed geographic areas in the world. According to the map, Brunei, China, Malaysia, the Philippines, Taiwan, and Vietnam have overlapping claims over the Spratly Islands. Thus, Choice *E* is the correct answer. Choice *A* is incorrect because only Taiwan challenges China's sovereign claim over Hainan. Choice *B* is incorrect because Kuala Lumpur is the capital of Malaysia. Although China, Taiwan, and Vietnam all claim the Paracel Islands, more states claim the Spratly Islands. As such, Choice *C* is incorrect. China, the Philippines, and Taiwan all claim sovereignty over the Scarborough Shoal, but this is also slightly less competitive than the battle over the Spratly Islands. Therefore, Choice *D* is incorrect.

7. E: The map depicts overlapping claims on the South China Sea. Based on the territorial scope of these claims, it can be inferred that they involve exclusive economic zones (EEZs). The United Nations Convention on the Law of the Sea (UNCLOS) grants states the right to establish EEZs within 200 nautical miles of their coasts. As such, the states implicated in this territorial dispute would cite UNCLOS to defend their claims under international law. Thus, Choice *E* is the correct answer. Brunei, Malaysia, the Philippines, and Vietnam are members of the Association of Southeast Asian Nations (ASEAN), and this supranational political organization has backed its members' claims. However, ASEAN is not directly involved in asserting or evaluating those claims, so Choice *A* is incorrect. Choice *B* is incorrect because the Convention on Facilitation of International Maritime Traffic (FAL Convention) concentrates on safeguarding and optimizing maritime travel. Choice *C* is incorrect because the International Convention for the Safety of Life at Sea (SOLAS) focuses on setting safety standards for ships. Choice *D* is incorrect because the International Maritime Organization (IMO) is a United Nations (UN) agency that regulates shipping.

8. B: Under the United Nations Convention on the Law of the Sea (UNCLOS), states may claim exclusive economic zones (EEZs) within 200 nautical miles of their coasts. Within EEZs, states enjoy commercial rights and privileges. For example, states can claim a monopoly over fisheries and oil deposits within their EEZs. Thus, Choice *B* is the correct answer. Choice *A* is somewhat correct in regard to the exploitation of maritime resources, but states are always obligated to provide foreign ships with the right to innocent passage under UNCLOS. As such, Choice *A* is incorrect. Choice *C* is incorrect because it states UNCLOS' definition of territorial waters. States are generally prohibited by maritime regions outside of their territorial sea, and China's construction of artificial islands in the South China Sea has been repeatedly challenged by the United States. So, Choice *D* is incorrect. States are allowed to enter

into bilateral international agreements to alter their political boundaries, but this practice isn't related to EEZs. Therefore, Choice E is incorrect.

9. A: Federal states feature a power-sharing arrangement between the central government and subnational government, whereas total sovereignty is vested in unitary states' central governments. Following a series of divisive cultural conflicts between Flanders and Wallonia, Belgium abandoned its unitary government and adopted a federal system of government. Thus, Choice A is the correct answer. China (Choice B), Egypt (Choice C), France (Choice D), and Saudi Arabia (Choice E) are incorrect because they are all unitary states. All four of these states have subnational units of government, but these states' central governments enjoy the power to overrule or abolish their subnational units.

10. A: The photograph is depicting a refugee camp. Centrifugal forces cause a breakdown in state sovereignty and societal harmony. The resulting chaos can lead to the persecution of stateless nations, and members are often forced to relocate to refugee camps. Thus, Choice A is the correct answer. Centripetal forces are the opposite of centrifugal forces. As such, centripetal forces generally cause states to become more unified and stable, so Choice B is incorrect. Devolution occurs when states cede some degree of sovereignty to subnational units of government, and it can ultimately result in state disintegration. Although devolution can also lead to forced migrations and refugee camps, centrifugal forces are more closely linked to this human tragedy. As such, Choice C is incorrect. Technological challenges can challenge state sovereignty, but the relationship of these challenges to refugee camps is tangential at best. So, Choice D is incorrect. Shatterbelts are areas outside of the control of sovereign states, and foreign powers often fight for control of these regions. Therefore, Choice E is incorrect.

11. C: Sovereignty is government's ability to project political power and authority over its territories, and territoriality refers to people's cultural, economic, and historical connections to land. Political entities have sought to increase territoriality in order to unify the state and maintain sovereign claims. Thus, Choice C is the correct answer. Sovereignty isn't exclusively held by central governments. In federal states, the central government shares sovereignty with subnational units of government. So, Choice A is incorrect. Sovereignty is also closely related to territorial control, and territoriality is more strongly associated with people's connections to land than political organizations. As such, Choice B is incorrect. Choice D is incorrect because all states need to exercise sovereignty in order to have a functional government. Choice E is incorrect because sovereignty and territoriality are both connected to states' territorial claims.

12. D: The map depicts European members of the North Atlantic Treaty Organization (NATO), which is a military organization. NATO originally formed in the aftermath of World War II to protect against a Soviet invasion of Western Europe. Thus, Choice D is the correct answer. Free-trade organizations seek to reduce barriers to trade, such as tariffs and domestic subsidies, and NATO isn't involved in free trade. So, Choice A is incorrect. Likewise, NATO isn't similar to international financial organizations, such as the World Bank and International Monetary Fund. In general, international financial organizations facilitate investment and development projects. As such, Choice B is incorrect. Many NATO members participate in joint task forces on transnational challenges, especially terrorism. However, Choice D is the better answer because all of the highlighted countries are members, so Choice C is incorrect. Choice E is incorrect because NATO isn't an explicitly political organization. Aside from the title, it's clear that the map isn't depicting the European Union (EU) because Albania, Iceland, Norway, and Turkey aren't members of the EU.

13. C: Like most defense alliances, the North Atlantic Treaty Organization (NATO) involves a common defense agreement. In addition, NATO facilitates the transfer of sensitive technologies, such as digital communication tools and missile defense systems, between members. Thus, Choice *C* is the correct answer. NATO is a supranational organization, and membership requires the transfer of some sovereignty to the organization. For example, under NATO's common defense agreement, if one member is attacked, all members are legally obligated to join the conflict. So, Choice *A* is incorrect. NATO isn't directly involved with members' economic or political issues, so Choice *B* is incorrect. Similarly, Choice *D* is incorrect because NATO is more concerned with military issues than foreign direct investment. Although NATO members regularly discuss transnational challenges, it is not the states' primary motivation for joining the organization. As such, Choice *E* is incorrect.

14. D: Ethnic separatist movements can challenge state sovereignty and trigger devolution. More specifically, devolution can occur when ethnic separatist movements pressure the government for more autonomy, advocate for secession, and incite civil wars. Thus, Choice *D* is the correct answer. Although ethnic separatist movements have historically forced states to adopt a federal system of government or create new autonomous regions, they are not the foundation for subnational units of government. Subnational units of government typically have a constitutional basis in federal states, and the central government is the source of their power in unitary states. So, Choice *A* is incorrect. Ethnic separatist movements function as centrifugal forces, not centripetal forces, because they undermine state sovereignty and unity. As such, Choice *B* is incorrect. Although ethnic separatist movements sometimes appeal to the international community for support, this isn't usually their primary method of seeking state disintegration. These movements more frequently demand sovereignty and incite civil wars; therefore, Choice *C* is incorrect. Likewise, although federalism can defuse ethnic separatist movements, these movements have broader goals than merely securing a transition from unitary to federal systems of government. So, Choice *E* is incorrect.

15. B: Prior to redistricting, the two political parties have relatively equal support in all four voting districts. Afterward, Political Party 1 gained a decisive advantage in three political districts by packing most of Political Party 2's supporters into a single district. This manipulative redistricting practice is commonly referred to as *gerrymandering*. Thus, Choice *B* is the correct answer. Nearly all states require voting districts to have contiguous borders, and all of the districts depicted in the diagram are contiguous. However, contiguity isn't a manipulative practice, so Choice *A* is incorrect. If redistricting had occurred in accordance with the principle of partisan fairness, the voting districts wouldn't have significantly changed. In fact, Political Party 2 likely dominated the redistricting process in order to achieve such a partisan victory. Therefore, Choice *C* is incorrect. Choice *D* is incorrect because proportional representation is an electoral system, not a redistricting practice. Reapportionment involves conducting a regular census to determine how population changes have impacted representation, which can lead to redistricting. As such, reapportionment isn't necessarily manipulative, so Choice *E* is incorrect.

Agriculture and Rural Land-Use Patterns and Processes

Introduction to Agriculture

Physical geography can either limit or expand the number of agricultural practices that can effectively be implemented. Important aspects of physical geography with a direct impact on agricultural practices include climatic conditions, sunlight, air quality, landforms, soil makeup, water availability, natural resources, plants, and animals. There are two broad categories of agricultural practices—intensive farming practices and extensive farming practices. In general, when the physical geography can support a wide range of agricultural practices, including practices that produce a large crop yield, societies tend to adopt intensive farming practices. When the physical geography is less conducive for large-scale agriculture, extensive farming practices are typically implemented instead.

Agricultural Practices

A geographic area's climate and physical environment have a significant impact on the development of agricultural practices. In general, the physical environment and climate can augment, limit, or prohibit certain agricultural practices.

Intensive farming is defined by relatively high labor requirements, sizable capital investments, and high yields of agricultural product size per unit of land. This agricultural practice is most commonly implemented in areas with rich soil, consistent water supply, and temperate to tropical climates. Climatic conditions can have a significant impact on the variety of crops that can be produced in an area. For example, bananas, cocoa, coffee, palm, and sugarcane can be grown in tropical climates but are difficult to cultivate in temperate climates. The Mediterranean region is another example of unique climatic conditions. This region has winter rains and summer droughts, which are ideal conditions for producing citrus fruits, olives, and grapes. In contrast, the Mediterranean climatic region is less suitable for animal husbandry because shallow root plants (grass) struggle to survive the seasonal droughts.

Although **extensive farming** requires less labor and capital than intensive farming, extensive farming typically requires a relatively large area of land. Additionally, extensive farming is extremely flexible in terms of its relationship to climatic conditions. For example, extensive farming is widely practiced in desert regions that cannot support agriculture due to a lack of water.

Intensive Farming Practices

The most common types of **intensive farming practices** are market gardening, mixed crop/livestock systems, and large-scale plantation agricultural systems. Market gardening is the cultivation of fruits, vegetables, and flowers. Although market gardening can occur on a relatively large plot of land, such as a family farm, this practice incorporates gardening techniques and intensive manual labor. Mixed crop/livestock systems, as the name suggests, produce a wide variety of plant and animal products. These systems tend to be sustainable because mixed cultivation strengthens nutrient cycling in the soil. Plantation agriculture specializes in profitable crops cultivated through large-scale production. As such, this practice requires a large supply of labor and significant capital investment. Examples of crops commonly grown in plantation agriculture include cocoa, cotton, coffee, rubber trees, sugarcane, and tobacco.

Extensive Farming Practices

Popular **extensive farming practices** are nomadic herding, ranching, and shifting cultivation. Nomadic herding involves the continual and irregular movement of livestock to fresh pastures. This practice is most commonly adopted when there's a lack of arable land, such as the steppe lands of Central Asia. Examples of livestock used in nomadic herding include goats, horses, llamas, sheep, water buffalo, and yaks. Ranching is similar to nomadic herding, but the livestock are moved between a central location and large pastures. In the present day, although most pastures are privately owned, some countries continue to operate public pastures called **commons**. Cattle, sheep, and horses are the most common ranch animals. Shifting cultivation is the temporary use of land for agriculture. After some period of time, farmers abandon the land and move their agricultural operation. This practice is most common in developing countries in regions where the soil won't support intensive agriculture.

Settlement Patterns and Survey Methods

Rural settlement patterns are clustered, dispersed, or linear and can readily be identified on maps by their patterns. Clustered settlements have a central focal point; dispersed settlements are scattered; and linear settlements appear along a line. Examples of popular rural survey methods include survey long lot, metes and bounds, and township and range. Geographers typically analyze rural settlements with the method used during the settlement's development.

Specific Agricultural Practices

Specific agricultural practices create distinct land-use patterns. Intensive farming involves plots of arable land used to produce crops on a seasonal or annual basis. These plots of land tend to be specifically defined, allowing for the development of a planned residential and/or commercial community at a central location among the plots. In contrast, extensive farming can involve less consistent land-use patterns because it generally involves shifting cultivation or pastures. Both intensive farming and extensive farming can alter the geographic landscape through the consumption and destruction of natural resources. Likewise, the construction of complex irrigation systems and canals for natural purposes alters natural waterways.

Rural Settlement Patterns

There are three different types of **rural settlement patterns**—clustered, dispersed, and linear. **Clustered rural settlement patterns** are typically highly planned, and they revolve around a central focal point. Historically, the central focal point was a religious or government institution; however, clustered rural settlements can also be based around a commercial center, transportation hub, housing development, or some other popular structure. In clustered rural settlements, agricultural production occurs in the area surrounding the focal point. **Dispersed rural settlement patterns** developed naturally over time without central planning and are generally marked by a series of scattered farms and pastures. Compared to clustered rural settlements, dispersed rural settlements tend to have more isolated communities. **Linear rural settlement patterns** involve structures built on a line, which can be either man-made or a natural barrier. For example, linear rural settlements often develop along a main road.

Rural Survey Methods

Geographers use three different methods when conducting rural surveys—long lot, metes and bounds, and township and range. The **long lot method** began with French colonial settlements in the Americas, such as Quebec and Louisiana. To simplify and clarify territorial claims, the French government granted "long lots" of land that were connected to waterfronts or roadways. The **metes and bounds survey method** is British in origin, and it remains popular in former British colonies, including Australia, India, Ontario (Canada), South Africa, and states in the eastern region of the United States. Metes and bounds create parcels of land based on narrative descriptions that use natural and man-made features, directions, and distances to define boundaries. Finally, **township and ranges surveys** originated in the

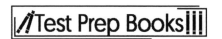

United States and use a grid pattern to divide land into survey townships. The lines running east-west are referred to as **townships**, and the lines running north-south are called **ranges**. Survey townships are approximately thirty-six square miles in size, meaning the township and range boundary lines are six miles long. In addition, survey townships can be further subdivided into thirty-six sections of one square mile parcels of land.

Agricultural Origins and Diffusions

The **domestication of plants and animals** occurred in hearths, meaning a place of origin. The major agricultural hearths developed in the Fertile Crescent (present-day Jordan, Iraq, Israel, Lebanon, and Syria); the Indus River Valley (present-day India and Pakistan); Southeast Asia (present-day Myanmar and Vietnam); and Mesoamerica (present-day El Salvador, Guatemala, Honduras, Mexico, Nicaragua, and Panama). The domestication of plants and animals in these agricultural hearths led to the **First Agricultural Revolution (Neolithic Revolution)**, which featured a shift from hunter-gatherer societies to agricultural societies.

Early Hearths of Domestication of Plants and Animals

The domestication of plants and animals first occurred in the Fertile Crescent. Grains of rye dating back to 11,000 BCE are the earliest evidence of a human society's domestication of plants. Ancient Syrians cultivated wild strands of rye to create a domesticated rye grain, which was used to make flour and bread. By 9,000 BCE, ancient civilizations in the Fertile Crescent had domesticated several annual cereal crops, including legumes and grains. The most common domesticated crops in this period were barley, peas, and wheat. The Fertile Crescent also played a leading role in the domestication of animals, such as pigs, sheep, and cattle.

Similar domestication efforts also occurred outside of the Fertile Crescent. The Indus River Valley domesticated red dates in approximately 9,000 BCE, and this was followed by the domestication of cattle, sheep, goats, and elephants. In addition, ancient Indian civilizations domesticated cotton between 5,000 BCE and 4,000 BCE. Ancient societies in Southeast Asia domesticated chicken, millet, rice, and soy in approximately 6,000 BCE. Mesoamerican societies domesticated a number of species, including beans, cocoa, maize, squash, and turkey, in approximately 4,000 BCE.

How Plants and Animals Diffused Globally

Following an extended period of domestication, plants and animals spread globally through patterns of diffusion, including the Columbian Exchange and several agricultural revolutions. Global diffusion happened on a large-scale basis during the Columbian Exchange (1492–1800) as European exploration and trade patterns triggered the global diffusion of animals, plants, people, diseases, technology, and ideas. For example, by the late nineteenth century, global trade resulted in American potato crops becoming an agricultural staple in Europe, Africa, and Asia. England developed several groundbreaking techniques during the Second Agricultural Revolution (1650–1890), resulting in increases to the viability of various livestock and crops across Europe, Africa, and the Americas. Similarly, during the Green Revolution (1950–1970), the United States spearheaded the transfer of new crops and technologies to countries in the developing world, such as Mexico, India, and the Philippines.

Second Agricultural Revolution

The **Second Agricultural Revolution** began in Great Britain during the seventeenth century as farmers began applying new techniques and technologies to boost productivity, such as the Norfolk crop rotation, new swing ploughs, advanced land-use projects, and selective livestock breeding. The Norfolk crop rotation introduced a system of four rotations to restore the soil and eliminate pests. British engineers improved Dutch and Chinese swing ploughs by adding cast-iron plating and interchangeable parts, which reduced the cost and increased maneuverability. The British government helped farmers convert livestock pastures into arable land to increase the production of crops. Selective livestock breeding greatly improved the size of animals and quality of animal products.

New Technology
The Second Agricultural Revolution's innovative techniques and technologies caused the global food supply to soar to unprecedented levels, particularly after the innovations spread across Europe and the Americas during the eighteenth century. Overall, the caloric intake and nutritional quality of European and American diets improved, which increased average life expectancies. The larger and more secure food supply also supported population growth, especially in Europe. Because the Second Agricultural Revolution expanded the food supply without increasing the demands on labor, more people joined the urban labor force, which spurred industrialization.

Green Revolution

Consequences of Green Revolution
The **Green Revolution** (1950–1970) has had a dramatic impact on human populations and the environment. Positive consequences mostly related to increased global food security, especially in the developing world. The global human population has increased by approximately 5 billion since 1950. As such, without the Green Revolution, it's likely that famine and malnutrition would have resulted in millions, if not billions, of deaths. In addition to increasing the average caloric intake all over the world, high-yield crops and advanced land management practices have increased agricultural efficiency. Greater efficiency has theoretically increased humanity's capacity to preserve wilderness because less land is needed for agricultural purposes.

However, the Green Revolution has also produced severe negative consequences. Its emphasis on monocultures of cereals has reduced the nutritional quality of diets for some populations, especially in the developing world. In addition, the corporatization of agriculture has bankrupted many smallholding and landless farmers. Aside from needing to compete with large-scale corporate farms, corporations own the intellectual property rights to high-yield crops. Pesticides and land degradation have contributed to the steep decline in wild biodiversity and widespread habitat destruction. Furthermore, the Green Revolution is highly dependent on nonrenewable energy resources, which has contributed to climate change.

Agricultural Production Regions

Economic forces play a major role in agricultural production. Subsistence farming is mostly practiced out of necessity in the developing world. Subsistence farmers generally lack sufficient resources to engage in commercial farming, so they pursue subsistence farming to feed their families. In contrast, commercial farming is pursued entirely for profit. Economic forces can also help determine whether land is used for intensive or extensive farming based on which practice has the greater profit potential.

Agricultural Production Regions
Agricultural production regions can be generally classified based on the ratio of subsistence and commercial practices. Subsistence practices refer to farmers who primarily grow crops and raise livestock to feed their own families. However, some complex economic relationships develop as subsistence farmers trade some of the surplus to access tools, materials, and resources. Approximately

2 billion people in the world are employed as subsistence farmers, with the heaviest concentrations in rural parts of developing countries in Africa, Asia, and Latin America.

Commercial practices refer to for-profit agriculture, meaning the overwhelming bulk of agricultural products are sold at market. To maximize profits, commercial farmers typically engage in monoculture or monocropping. Monoculture is the concentrated production of a single agricultural product, whereas monocropping refers to the continuation of a monoculture into the next year and beyond. Monoculture and monocropping increase profits based on specialization and concentration on the most commercially valuable products. However, this agricultural practice can harm the environment through soil degradation and reduced agricultural biodiversity. Commercial agricultural production regions are most common in developed countries.

Bid-Rent Theory

The **bid-rent theory** is a major factor in determining whether farmers will engage in intensive or extensive farming practices. The guiding principle of the bid-rent theory is that people will pay higher rents to access more profitable areas of land. Under the bid-rent theory, profit motive functions as the organizing principle within the free market, arguably increasing the efficiency of land use because prices reflect potential value to the buyer.

Some land is more suitable to intensive farming or extensive farming. According to the bid-rent theory, this determination will be made based on profit potential. For example, fertile land in a moderate climate will be most conducive to intensive farming practices. As such, a prospective intensive farmer would value the land more than an extensive farmer due to the possibility of greater profits. Therefore, the intensive farmer would likely be more willing to pay a higher rent on the land than an extensive farmer.

Spatial Organization of Agriculture

Economics has a dramatic impact on agricultural practices. Agriculture has increasingly become big business, and small family farms are struggling to compete due to expensive technological innovations and economies of scale. These factors have dramatically transformed agricultural production in developed countries, and they're beginning to play a larger role in the developing world. Similarly, complex commodity chains within the global supply chain have forged economic relationships that connect agricultural production and consumption.

Large-Scale Commercial Agricultural Operations

Large-scale commercial farms have increasingly bankrupted small family farms since the Green Revolution. Although mechanization has contributed to exponential growth in terms of global agricultural productivity, it's prohibitively expensive. Unlike large-scale commercial farms, owners of small family farms cannot afford to deploy a fleet of the latest agricultural machines, such as tractors and combine harvesters. Likewise, the prices for pesticides, fertilizers, and genetically modified foods have increased because multinational corporations have consolidated control over the underlying intellectual property rights. For example, Monsanto-Bayer has achieved a near monopoly over genetically modified seeds, and the powerful corporation has repeatedly sued small farmers for unknowingly using seeds that naturally cross-pollinated with Monsanto-Bayer's proprietary crops.

The trend toward large-scale farming is most noticeable in developed countries in which agriculture is driven by efficiency. For example, in 2014, only 4 percent of American farms had more than $1 million in agricultural sales; however, those large-scale farms accounted for 66 percent of all agricultural sales in the United States. During that same time period, 75 percent of American farms had less than $50,000 in agricultural sales. Although small family farms remain the norm in much of the developing world, that is also starting to change. Many farmers in the developing world have sought to emulate developed countries' success in increasing agricultural production, and multinational corporations have also ventured into these markets for large-scale agricultural sourcing.

Complex Commodity Chains

The global supply chain for food and other agricultural products includes many **complex commodity chains** that connect production and consumption. Food companies rarely directly engage in the large-scale production of their ingredients. Instead, these companies engage in contract farming to create a commodity chain. Contract farming involves a contract for a specified amount of agricultural product that is needed to meet a designated quality standard and delivery timetable. Contract farms benefit from a guaranteed buyer and logistical support. In turn, the contracting company can mitigate risks by diversifying production among several contract farms. Finally, commodity chains might involve several layers of multiple contracts for a single food item, creating an interconnected web of economic relationships.

The complexity of contemporary commodity chains has been criticized for decreasing transparency and oversight over agricultural production. This has arguably exacerbated issues related to labor practices and/or environmental pollution. For example, Cargill, the largest privately held corporation in the United States, has faced fierce criticism for deforestation caused by its commodity chains for soy in Brazil, cocoa in the Ivory Coast, and palm oil in Sumatra and Borneo.

Technological Innovations

Technological innovations in agricultural production have increased the carrying capacity of land and economies of scale. The Green Revolution produced numerous technological innovations that have made agricultural production more efficient. More recently, large-scale farms have begun using airplanes, helicopters, computers, and satellite imagery to increase precision in monitoring crops. As a result, improved efficiency has increased the carrying capacity of the land, meaning more food can be grown per unit of land. Likewise, technology has increased economies of scale, meaning costs decrease as production increases. Economies of scale are a major reason why large-scale farms have outcompeted family farms. In effect, technological innovations have allowed farms with sufficient capital to rapidly expand and, due to economies of scale, earn more profits as their costs decrease.

Von Thünen Model

The **von Thünen model** allows geographers to analyze spatial economics by placing a theoretical city around four zones, depicted as concentric rings. The first zone includes dairy, fruit, and vegetable products. The second zone consists of timber and fuel products. The third zone features cereal crops and livestock ranching. The fourth zone is wilderness with limited economic purpose. Using the von Thünen model, geographers can analyze agricultural production at different scales based on a location's relative position to resources.

One of the von Thünen model's most important insights is its creation of zones based on transportation costs. The first zone includes products that expire most rapidly because they need to reach markets quickly. The second zone includes timber and fuel products, which must be produced relatively close to the city because they are heavy and difficult to transport. Finally, the third zone includes grains, field crops, and ranching livestock that can be placed the farthest away from the city because they are durable and/or easily transportable. This treatment of transportation costs is highly relevant for

analyzing rural land use, particularly in combination with the bid-rent theory. A notable exception to the von Thünen model is specialty farming products because they're dependent on specific climate and soil conditions.

Global System of Agriculture

The contemporary **global system of agriculture** is defined by its interdependence. Advances in infrastructure networks, refrigeration technologies, and free-trade agreements have led to the development of a complex global supply chain for food and other agricultural products. To varying degrees, every country is involved in producing, exporting, and importing food products through the global supply chain. However, the global supply chain can become tumultuous when faced with political disputes and severe weather events.

Food and Other Agricultural Products

A global supply chain currently connects the production, distribution, and consumption of food and other agricultural products through complex worldwide commercial networks. Although some products might be produced, distributed, and consumed in a single country, they are still impacted by the global supply chain's effect on pricing through the law of supply and demand. The only types of food production that fall outside of the global supply chain are subsistence farmers and hunter-gatherers because these groups consume what they produce.

There are four stages in the contemporary global supply chain for food and other agricultural products. The first stage involves the production of plants and animals, mostly through agriculture and commercial fishing. The second stage consists of processing food products, including both the packaging of fresh food products and the manufacturing of food products from raw ingredients. The third stage relates to distribution, meaning how food moves from the site of production to marketplaces. Often, distribution requires the transportation and warehousing of products at multiple places before reaching their eventual final destination. Refrigeration techniques played a critical role in creating the global supply chain because it allowed fresh food products to be transported all over the world. The fourth stage is the marketplace, such as grocery stores, wholesale retailers, farmers' markets, and restaurants. Grocery stores are particularly important because they sell a multitude of fresh products and manufactured products from all over the world.

Export Commodities

Although all countries import food to varying degrees, some countries are entirely dependent on importing food products. The three most common reasons for countries' overreliance on export commodities are an inhospitable climate, armed conflict, and lack of access to mechanized equipment and other agricultural technologies. For example, in the 2010s, Afghanistan suffered from food insecurity due to a prolonged armed conflict that exacerbated the devastation caused by seasonal droughts and flooding. Consequently, Afghanistan's food supply effectively depends on importing wheat flour from neighboring countries. As a region, sub-Saharan Africa suffers the highest rates of food insecurity in the world, and the region would face famine-like conditions if it didn't import massive amounts of wheat and rice.

Infrastructure, Patterns of World Trade, and Political Relationships

Infrastructure, patterns of world trade, and political relationships impact global food distribution networks. Trucks, ships, and airplanes conduct global food distribution, and when transportation occurs across long distances, all of these methods must be outfitted with cold chain logistical systems (refrigeration and/or freezing). Additionally, countries need to maintain the requisite roadways, docks,

and airports to facilitate transportation. Patterns of world trade are most heavily influenced by free-trade agreements. Under these agreements, countries agree to mutually reduce barriers to trade. Often, this can force countries to sacrifice domestic industries. For example, despite having its own robust dairy industry, Canada imports dairy products from the United States in order to secure more favorable terms for its exports, such as fossil fuels. However, free-trade relationships require maintaining political relationships, and if broken, it can disrupt distribution. For example, in 2018, a growing trade war between the United States and China led to Chinese importers purchasing soybeans from Brazil, dealing a serious blow to many American farmers.

Consequences of Agricultural Practices

Agricultural practices have substantial environmental and societal consequences. On one extreme, agricultural practices can pollute the natural environment, trigger land cover change, and destroy ecosystems. Specifically, plantations and large-scale livestock operations are the leading cause of habitat destruction and pollution. However, some agricultural practices are sustainable, such as agricultural terracing and shifting cultivation. Societal consequences include dietary improvements, increased female participation in agricultural production, and agriculture functioning as a way of life for communities.

Environmental Effects

Agriculture land use has a number of harmful environmental effects, including pollution, land cover change, desertification, soil salinization, and conservation efforts. **Agricultural pollution** is any by-product of agricultural production that contaminates, degrades, or otherwise harms the environment, and it has many forms. For example, pesticides regularly kill unintended organisms, and fertilizer runoff can contaminate the groundwater. **Land cover change** refers to how areas of agricultural production displace natural areas, destroying ecosystems and reducing biodiversity. **Desertification** is an unintentional type of land cover change. When agricultural production overexploits soil nutrients, "soil death" can occur, causing the land to transform into a desert. Desertification poses the greatest threat to arid areas. **Soil salinization** occurs when irrigation and fertilization raise salinity levels. Once salinity levels pass a certain threshold, only salt-tolerant soil will be able to survive, and the land will be vulnerable to desertification. Many **conservation efforts** have been launched to protect the natural environment from agriculture. Some activists have called for more sustainable agricultural production, such as replacing plantations with mixed crop/livestock systems. Other activists pursue government regulations and commercial boycotts to protect the environment.

Agricultural Practices Alter the Landscape

Many agricultural practices, such as deforestation, irrigation, draining wetlands, terracing, shifting cultivation, slash and burn, and pastoral nomadism, change the natural landscape. **Deforestation** is the elimination of forests for commercial or residential purposes, and this practice destroys ecosystems, reduces biodiversity, and worsens climate change. **Irrigation** refers to the diversion of water for commercial purposes, such as intensive agriculture. Modern irrigation systems can control the amount of water and how it's distributed. Irrigation sometimes results in the **draining of wetlands** as the water is redistributed to farmland. Additionally, draining wetlands is often intentionally done to increase arable land.

Agricultural terracing involves placing crops on a slope featuring a series of step platforms, and it has been practiced for more than one thousand years in hilly and mountainous regions. Terraces are a sustainable form of agricultural production because they reduce erosion, decrease surface runoff, and

require less irrigation. **Shifting cultivation** refers to abandoning areas of agricultural production until the soil is restored. **Slash-and-burn agriculture** is a subtype of shifting cultivation that involves burning wooded area or forests to create a field. The ash functions as a natural fertilizer, and once the field is no longer productive, it is abandoned. **Pastoral nomadism** is another term for nomadic herding, and it involves the continual and irregular movement to fresh pastures. This practice can lead to desertification when the livestock overgrazes.

Societal Effects of Agricultural Practices

Modern agricultural practices have three primary societal effects. First, the Green Revolution and global supply chains have combined to change diets across the world. In general, diets for most populations are significantly more diverse, with higher nutritional caloric content when compared to the beginning of the twentieth century. Second, women play a sizable role in agricultural production, especially in the developing world. In some regions, such as sub-Saharan Africa, women account for more than 50 percent of agricultural production. Third, agriculture provides an economic purpose for an overwhelming number of people. Approximately 28 percent of the global population is directly employed in agricultural production, and 60 percent of the global population depends on subsistence farming for survival.

Challenges of Contemporary Agriculture

Agricultural production and consumption have rapidly changed in recent years, leading to numerous debates. Although biotechnology, genetically modified organisms (GMOs), and aquacultures have helped expand the food supply, they're criticized over environmental sustainability concerns. Agricultural production faces countless economic challenges, and consumer-based movements have prioritized nutritional value and sustainable production, creating opportunities for relatively small farms. Furthermore, distribution suffers from inefficiencies that lead to food insecurity and food deserts developing all over the world.

Agricultural Innovations

Biotechnologies, GMOs, and aquaculture are among the most hotly debated agricultural innovations. **Biotechnologies** have allowed scientists to develop numerous genetically modified crops, and the practice is widespread. For example, more than 90 percent of American soy and corn crops have undergone genetic modification. The modification of crops' genetic material is usually intended to extend shelf life, improve nutritional value, and increase resiliency during cultivation. Likewise, scientists currently leverage biotechnology to improve the health of livestock, and many genetically modified animals are currently in development.

Advocates for biotechnologies and **genetically modified organisms (GMOs)** argue that these advancements eliminate extensive fertilizer and pesticide use. In addition, genetic modification increases efficiency in cultivation, and therefore there will be less stress on soil and water usage. In response, critics argue that GMOs reduce biodiversity of crops, which could exponentially increase the harm of a crop failure. Critics further assert that GMOs promote monocropping on large-scale agricultural operations, which is not environmentally sustainable. Finally, there are economic issues related to corporate ownership of GMOs.

Aquaculture refers to the farming of fish and other maritime organisms. Rather than harvesting wild fish, the farming of fish involves stocking and cultivating a specific population that's commercially owned. Economists estimate that aquacultures currently account for more than 50 percent of global fish and shellfish consumption. Advocates argue that this practice is necessary because wild fisheries have experienced a sharp decline in recent decades. However, aquacultures face criticism for destroying coastal ecosystems, creating inefficiencies in production, increasing maritime levels of pesticides and antibiotics, and reducing biodiversity through the accidental introduction of invasive species.

Patterns of Food Production and Consumption

Various consumer-led movements about food choice have altered patterns of food production and consumption. Dietary shifts have increased the demand for new types of food, such as vegetarian, vegan, and gluten-free products. Urban farming has led to the cultivation of fruits and vegetables within major cities around the world. Value-added specialty crops have increased the economic value of an agricultural product through changes to production, processing, or marketing.

Organic farming produces foods with fewer pesticides and fertilizers, and the end product typically doesn't contain synthetic additives. Numerous countries and trade associations issue certifications for organic foods that meet specific criteria. There has also been a growing demand for agricultural products with fair-trade certification. Several trade organizations label products as fair trade if they meet certain labor and environmental standards in their production. Likewise, local food movements have increased in popularity as consumers place higher premiums on environmental sustainability. Compared to large-scale agricultural operations, family farms tend to produce products in a more sustainable manner, and buying local reduces pollution caused by distribution across long distances. Community-supported agriculture (CSA) is a specific type of local food movement that directly connects producers and consumers through a subscription model.

Feeding a Global Population

There are numerous challenges to **feeding a global population**. Adverse weather regularly destabilizes the global supply chain for agricultural products, and scientists project extreme weather events to increase in frequency due to climate change. Other problems relate to the role of the profit motive in food production and distribution. In a free market system adhering to the bid-rent theory, significant amounts of agricultural land are lost due to an expansion of high-priced suburban homes. As a result, agricultural production has been physically separated from communities to an unprecedented extent.

Many developing countries suffer from systemic and endemic food insecurity, meaning a lack of nutritious and affordable food, due to poverty and lack of access to agricultural technologies. Numerous developed countries also have serious issues with food insecurity. For example, in 2018, approximately 11 million children suffered from food insecurity in the United States. Food deserts—areas with limited access to fresh food (supermarkets)—are also a chronic problem in both the developed and developing world. Approximately 23 million Americans live in a food desert.

Economic Effects on Food Production Practices

Several factors have an economic effect on food production practices. Distribution systems often have extensive requirements for travel logistics and delivery timelines, especially when production occurs far away from food processing plants and marketplaces. As a result, delays in production can be catastrophic because falling out of sync with a distribution system can lead to lower sale prices or a ruined harvest. Countless government policies can influence the economics of food production, ranging from regulations on agrochemicals to zoning laws. Finally, economies of scale push farms to expand production because expansion reduces the cost of production, increasing profits.

Women in Agriculture

Female roles in food production and consumption exhibit considerable geographic variation, and the differences are often tied to stages of economic development. Female contribution to food production is highest in the developing world. Most developing countries have an agricultural workforce composed of at least 30 percent women. Sub-Saharan Africa has the highest female contribution to food production, with most countries exceeding 50 percent participation. Compared to developing countries, the United States and Europe have significantly lower female participation in food production. Female roles in consumption are more consistent in developing and developed countries due to the prevalence of traditional societal roles. Women are statistically more likely to be involved in childrearing and food consumption in most societies. However, women in developed countries have relatively smaller roles in food consumption, largely because they are more likely to be employed outside the home.

Female roles in food production, distribution, and consumption are directly affected by type of agricultural production. Most women engaged in food production and distribution participate in intensive farming. In contrast, extensive farming is more likely to be a male-dominated field due to its migratory characteristics. Women are most likely to play a leading role in food production, distribution, and consumption in subsistence farming, especially in sub-Saharan Africa.

Practice Questions

Question 1 refers to the map below.

Rural Population Density Map

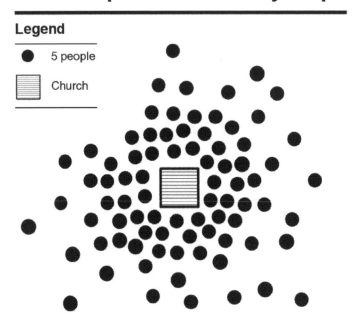

Legend

●   5 people

▨   Church

1. The map depicts which of the following types of rural settlement pattern?
   - a. Clustered
   - b. Dispersed
   - c. Linear
   - d. Long Lot
   - e. Religious

2. Which of the following agricultural practices requires a massive supply of cheap labor and involves large-scale monocropping?
   - a. Extensive farming
   - b. Market gardening
   - c. Mixed agricultural system
   - d. Plantation agriculture
   - e. Shifting cultivation

Questions 3 and 4 refer to the diagram below.

Patterns of Diffusion, circa 1600

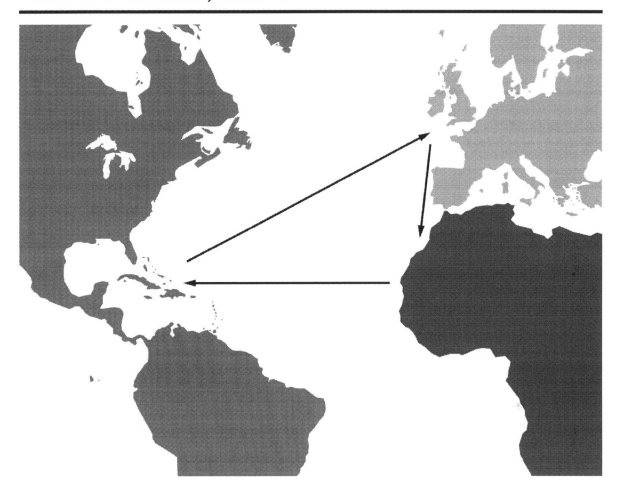

3. The diagram most likely illustrates which of the following patterns of diffusion?
    a. Columbian Exchange
    b. Contemporary global supply chain
    c. Free-trade network
    d. Green Revolution
    e. Second Agricultural Revolution

4. Which of the following most accurately describes the consequence of this pattern of diffusion?
    a. The pattern of diffusion led to the corporatization of agricultural production, resulting in economic catastrophe for small family farms.
    b. The pattern of diffusion resulted in the spread of the Norfolk crop rotation techniques and new iron swing ploughs.
    c. The pattern of diffusion generated new employment opportunities, disproportionately benefiting low-income communities.
    d. The pattern of diffusion initiated the beginning of European colonization in the Americas and Africa, which increased and diversified the food supply in European countries.
    e. The pattern of diffusion triggered groundbreaking global diffusion of agricultural products.

5. Which of the following is NOT a negative environmental effect of large-scale agricultural operations?
    a. Conservationism
    b. Deforestation
    c. Desertification
    d. Land cover change
    e. Soil salinization

Questions 6 and 7 refer to the diagram below.

Urban Development Diagram

6. The diagram depicts which of the following models of urban development?
    a. Bid-rent theory
    b. Galactic city model
    c. Harris and Ullman multiple-nuclei model
    d. Rostow's Stages of Economic Growth
    e. Von Thünen model

7. Within the circle labeled "1," which of the following is most likely being produced?
    a. Cereal crops
    b. Fruit
    c. Fuel
    d. Livestock
    e. Timber

8. Which of the following most accurately summarizes the criticism of genetically modified organisms?
   a. Genetically modified organisms have an inferior shelf life compared to natural farm crops.
   b. Genetically modified organisms provide insufficient nutritional value.
   c. Genetically modified organisms decrease biodiversity.
   d. Genetically modified organisms aren't compatible with large-scale agricultural operations.
   e. Genetically modified organisms always require more soil and water during cultivation.

9. Customers order a recurring monthly shipment of fresh vegetables from local farmers. Which of the following patterns of food consumption and production does this example describe?
   a. Agricultural surplus
   b. Community-supported agriculture
   c. Fair trade
   d. Local food movements
   e. Urban farming

Question 10 refers to the picture below.

Packaged Coffee

10. Which of the following best describes how this product was produced?
   a. Production occurred on a local family farm that prioritizes environmental sustainability.
   b. Production occurred through a partnership with a worker-owned cooperative.
   c. Production met environmental sustainability standards and included reasonable compensation to workers.
   d. Production abided by free-trade rules, resulting in reduced costs for consumers.
   e. Production directly connected producers and consumers, circumventing the control of multinational corporations.

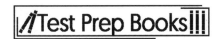

Question 11 refers to the chart below.

Annual Agricultural Output of a Farm

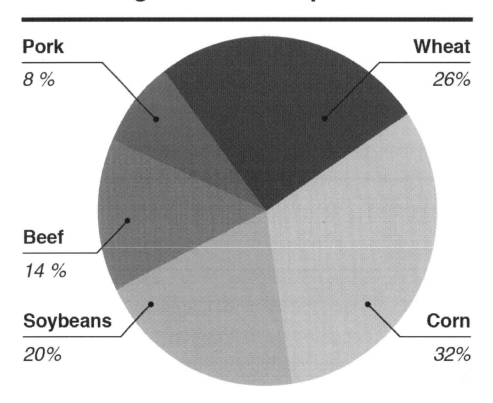

Pork 8 %

Wheat 26%

Beef 14 %

Soybeans 20%

Corn 32%

11. Based on the pie chart, the farm is most likely engaged in which of the following methods of agricultural production?
   a. Extensive farming
   b. Market gardening
   c. Mixed crop/livestock system
   d. Plantation agriculture
   e. Ranching

12. Economies of scale result in reduced costs as agricultural production increases. Which of the following best describes the negative consequences of this trend?
   a. Economies of scale have removed incentives for developing agricultural innovations.
   b. Economies of scale have promoted extensive farming practices to the detriment of small family farms.
   c. Economies of scale have disrupted global commodity chains, shifting the costs of production onto consumers.
   d. Economies of scale have spurred the corporatization of agriculture, bankrupting small family farms.
   e. Economies of scale have prevented the development of new food production and consumption movements.

Questions 13 and 14 refer to the map below.

Rural Survey

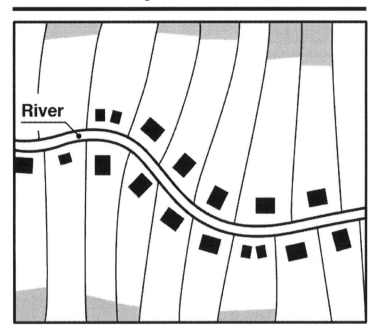

13. The map is depicting which of the following rural survey methods?
    a. Field studies
    b. Government census
    c. Metes and bounds
    d. Long Lot
    e. Township and range

14. Where did this survey method originate?
    a. England
    b. France
    c. India
    d. South Africa
    e. United States

15. Farmers build step platforms on a mountainous slope to decrease surface runoff and reduce the demand for irrigation. This example describes which of the following agricultural practices?
    a. Market gardening
    b. Pastoral nomadism
    c. Shifting cultivation
    d. Slash-and-burn agriculture
    e. Terrace agriculture

Answer Explanations

1. A: The map has a church surrounded by a large concentration of dots. According to the legend, each dot represents five people. There are other dots on the map, but they're distributed sporadically. Clustered settlements have a central focal point where population density is the highest, and this matches the scenario expressed on the map. Choice *B* is incorrect because dispersed rural settlements don't have a central focal point, and they tend to have sporadic population distribution. Choice *C* is incorrect because linear settlements are built along a man-made or natural barrier, and the population distribution looks like a relatively straight line. Choice *D* is incorrect because long lots are a rural survey method, not a rural settlement pattern. Choice *E* is incorrect. It is a red herring. Although the church functions as a central focal point, rural settlement patterns are not classified based on the presence of a religious institution.

2. D: Plantation agriculture is a form of intensive agriculture that specializes in the large-scale production of crops for commercial purposes. In order to achieve the necessary economies of scale, plantation agriculture requires a massive supply of labor. Additionally, a plantation agricultural operation concentrates on producing the most profitable crop, so monocropping is common. Monocropping refers to the continual production of a single crop. Choice *A* is incorrect; extensive farming practices, such as nomadic herding and shifting cultivation, don't require a large labor supply because these practices don't involve large-scale production. Choice *B* is incorrect because market gardening focuses on growing a variety of fruits, vegetables, and flowers and doesn't involve monocropping. Choice *C* is incorrect because although mixed agricultural systems can require a large labor supply, this agricultural practice doesn't engage in monocropping. By definition, mixed agricultural systems involve the production of several crops and livestock. Choice *E* is incorrect because shifting cultivation involves the temporary use of land for agricultural purposes. This agricultural practice is flexible and doesn't depend on a large labor supply.

3. A: The diagram has a series of arrows pointing from the Americas to Europe, Europe to Africa, and Africa to the Americas. This pattern is consistent with the Columbian Exchange. During the colonization of the Americas, Europeans transported African slaves to the Americas, extracted raw resources from the Americas, and exported manufactured goods to Africa. Choice *B* is incorrect because the title of the map says it represents a pattern of diffusion that was active in the seventeenth century, and the contemporary global supply chain includes Asia and Australia. Similarly, Choice *C* is incorrect because free-trade networks weren't active in the seventeenth century. Choice *D* is incorrect because the Green Revolution involved the diffusion of high-yield crops and technological innovations during the mid-twentieth century. Likewise, Choice *E* is incorrect because the Second Agricultural Revolution featured the diffusion of groundbreaking agricultural techniques and technologies during the eighteenth century.

4. E: The pattern of diffusion can be identified as the Columbian Exchange due to the time period and emphasis on Europe, Africa, and the Americas. The Columbian Exchange included a significant diffusion of agricultural products. For example, merchants exported the American potato to Europe, and it quickly became a staple crop. Choice *A* is incorrect because small family farms thrived during the Columbian Exchange, and the corporatization of agricultural production didn't occur until the latter half of the twentieth century. Choice *B* is incorrect because the Norfolk crop rotation and iron swing plough spread from England to the Americas during the Second Agricultural Revolution in the eighteenth century. Choice *C* is incorrect because although the Columbian Exchange did generate new employment opportunities in international commerce, the economic activity enriched states and wealthy investors. As such, low-income communities weren't the primary beneficiaries. Choice *D* is incorrect because

although the Columbian Exchange did increase and diversify the European food supply, colonization predated its formation by more than a century. European colonization began shortly after Christopher Columbus arrived in the Caribbean in 1492.

5. A: Conservationism prioritizes protecting the natural environment, including protection from the harm caused by large-scale agricultural operations. Choice *B* is incorrect because large-scale agricultural operations, such as plantation agriculture and ranching, can have devastating consequences for the environment. The clearing of forests for farmland and grazing pastures is known as deforestation, and it can destroy ecosystems and reduce biodiversity. Choice *C* is incorrect because large-scale agricultural operations can overexploit soil nutrients, and if the nutrients are depleted, arable land will transform into a desert in a process referred to as *desertification*. Choice *D* is incorrect because land cover change occurs when agricultural operations displace natural ecosystems, resulting in habitat destruction. Choice *E* is incorrect because large-scale application of irrigation techniques and fertilizers can lead to soil salinization, which kills plants that can't tolerate elevated salinity levels.

6. E: The diagram has five concentric circles, and the circle at the center is labeled "Urban Core." Geographers use the von Thünen model to analyze spatial economics at play in urban development. Choice *A* is incorrect; the bid-rent theory is somewhat related to the von Thünen model because profitability functions as an organizing principle. For example, vegetable farmers are willing to pay higher rents to be in the concentric circle closest to the "Urban Core" so they can quickly bring their products to market. However, the bid-rent theory doesn't feature a model with concentric circles. Choice *B* is incorrect because the galactic city model organizes economic zones and cities based on their economic relationships, and the model looks like a constellation of stars. Choice *C* is incorrect; the Harris and Ullman multiple-nuclei model theorizes that there are multiple centers of economic production that internal structures develop around. The diagram organizes economic sectors around a single "Urban Core." Choice *D* is incorrect because Rostow's Stages of Economic Growth describe a linear trajectory from a traditional society to a developed country, not urban development.

7. B: Outside of the "Urban Core," the von Thünen model arranges the next three concentric circles based on the transportation costs for various sectors. The economic sector labeled "1" on the diagram is the closest to the "Urban Core," and it includes agricultural products that need to get to market quickly before expiring, such as dairy and fruit. Choices *A* and *D* are both incorrect because cereal crops and livestock are more durable and easily transportable, and therefore the von Thünen model arranges these agricultural products in the concentric circle labeled "3" on the diagram. Choices *C* and *E* are both incorrect because fuel and timber are heavy and relatively difficult to transport, and therefore the von Thünen model places them in the concentric circle labeled "2" on the diagram.

8. C: Genetically modified organisms are designed to increase shelf life, add nutritional value, and improve resiliency. On the one hand, they have dramatically increased the global food supply in an efficient manner. However, genetically modified organisms are criticized for several reasons. One criticism is that genetically modified organisms decrease biodiversity. For example, approximately 90 percent of American corn crops are genetically modified organisms, and they have replaced natural crops. Choice *A* is incorrect because genetically modified organisms generally have a longer, not shorter, shelf life than natural crops. Choice *B* is incorrect because genetically modified organisms typically have the same or greater nutritional value compared to natural crops. Choice *D* is incorrect because genetically modified organisms are frequently produced on large-scale agricultural operations. Choice *E* is incorrect because genetically modified organisms can often be cultivated with less water and soil nutrients than natural crops.

9. B: The prompt describes customers ordering monthly shipments from local farmers. Community-supported agriculture directly connects agricultural producers and consumers in this way, usually through a subscription model. Choice *A* is incorrect because an agricultural surplus is the amount of production that surpasses society's needs, and therefore it is typically exported to a foreign market or stored for later use. Choice *C* is incorrect because fair trade is a certification for products that meet specific environmental and labor standards. Choice *D* is incorrect because although the prompt mentions local farmers, local food movements don't necessarily involve a direct relationship between producers and consumers. Choice *E* is incorrect because urban farming refers to the cultivation of agricultural products within an urban environment.

10. C: The product in the image has a "Fair Trade" label. Trade organizations certify products as fair trade when they are produced in accordance with specific labor and environmental standards. The environmental standards always emphasize sustainability, and labor standards typically include reasonable compensation to workers. Choice *A* is incorrect because although environmental sustainability is part of the fair-trade movement, the production of these certified products doesn't necessarily occur on family farms. Choice *B* is incorrect because although many worker-owned cooperatives produce fair-trade agricultural products, this isn't a requirement for certification. Choice *D* is incorrect because fair trade isn't related to free trade, and consumers typically pay a premium for fair-trade products. Choice *E* is incorrect because it describes community-supported agriculture, which isn't required for fair-trade certification.

11. C: The pie chart includes a fairly wide range of agricultural products. None of the products account for more than a third of the farm's annual agricultural output. Mixed crop/livestock systems feature a variety of agricultural crops and livestock. Choice *A* is incorrect; extensive farming is a broad category of agricultural practices, such as nomadic herding, ranching, and shifting cultivation. Shifting cultivation can involve a variety of crops, but the practice doesn't typically involve livestock. Choice *B* is incorrect because market gardening applies gardening techniques to growing fruits, vegetables, and flowers on farmland. Livestock isn't a key component of market gardening. Choice *D* is incorrect because plantation agriculture generally involves monocropping but not raising livestock. Choice *E* is incorrect because ranching involves livestock but not the cultivation of crops.

12. D: Economies of scale have encouraged farms to continually expand operations, and most recently, this had led to corporatization. Unlike corporations, small family farms don't have the capital to purchase more land and invest in the latest technological innovations. Due to this discrepancy, small family farms aren't able to compete with large-scale operations in terms of the prices they can offer customers. In the face of these challenges, many small family farms have declared bankruptcy. Choice *A* is incorrect because economies of scale incentivize the development of innovations due to the greater potential for profit. Choice *B* is incorrect; large-scale operations practice intensive agriculture, not extensive agriculture, because it is more profitable. Choice *C* is incorrect because economies of scale are the central feature of contemporary global commodity chains, and this scheme generally drives down prices for consumers. Choice *E* is incorrect because many new food production and consumption movements have developed in response to the rise of large-scale agricultural operations, such as community-supported agriculture, local food movements, and urban farming.

13. D: The map depicts rectangular parcels of land extending away from a river, which is characteristic of the long lot survey method. Long lots date back to European colonization, and the land parcels were organized based on a physical connection to waterfronts and roadways for purposes of simplicity. Choice *A* is incorrect because field reports are a method of collecting qualitative data, not a rural survey method. Choice *B* is incorrect because a government census is used to collect quantitative data.

Although a government census can be used to conduct a rural survey, the diagram specifically depicts the long lot method. Choice *C* is incorrect because the metes and bounds survey method uses narrative descriptions, directions, and distances to define boundaries for land parcels. Additionally, these parcels aren't necessarily rectangular or connected to a natural or man-made feature. Choice *E* is incorrect because the township and range survey method uses a grid pattern that doesn't resemble anything on the diagram.

14. B: The diagram is illustrating the long lot survey method, and it originated in France. The French government used the long lot survey method to organize land grants to colonists in the Americas. Choice *A* is incorrect because the metes and bounds survey method, not the long lot survey method, originated in England. Choices *C* and *D* are both incorrect because these countries are former British colonies, and therefore they used the metes and bounds survey method. Choice *E* is incorrect because although the long lot survey is currently used in some parts of the United States, such as Louisiana, it didn't originate there. The United States created the metes and bounds survey method.

15. E: The prompt mentions step platforms on a mountainous slope, which matches terrace agriculture. Farmers have engaged in terrace agriculture for centuries because it is sustainable and relatively simple. Terrace agriculture can decrease erosion, surface runoff, and irrigation requirements. Choice *A* is incorrect because market gardening applies gardening techniques to agricultural production. Choice *B* is incorrect because pastoral nomadism involves continually moving livestock to fresh pasture in an irregular pattern. Choice *C* is incorrect because shifting cultivation refers to using land for agricultural purposes until it's no longer productive and then abandoning it. Choice *D* is incorrect because slash-and-burn agriculture is a type of shifting agriculture, and it involves burning forests to create a natural fertilizer.

Cities and Urban Land-Use Patterns and Processes

Origin and Influences of Urbanization

Urbanization occurs as population density increases, resulting in more complex and interrelated socioeconomic relationships. As a result, urban areas often experience significant economic growth, which attracts migrants. Population and economic growth patterns can combine to form a virtuous cycle, fueling further innovation in urbanization. Transportation and communication innovations can also lead to the suburbanization of outlying areas. Additionally, rapid increases to population density can increase the trend toward suburbanization as wealthier inhabitants seek more sanitary and spacious living conditions. In general, suburbs retain strong economic, social, and political ties to the city.

Site and Situation

Site and situation have an immense impact on the development of cities. **Site** is the actual location of a city, covering the land on which the city has been built. **Situation** is a related concept, and it refers to the city's relationship to surrounding areas, including both man-made and natural features. Many settlements first developed at a strategic location. For example, city planners originally built Rome on a hilltop for defensive purposes, and the city's situation benefited the city based on the proximity to waterways and arable land in the surrounding area. Similarly, site and situation influence the function of cities. The concentration of urban populations provides cities with disproportionately greater economic, political, and social influence compared to rural areas. As such, the site of cities often functions as the central focus of socioeconomic and political systems, and in turn, this centrality leads to changes in cities' situations as suburbs develop in the surrounding areas. Likewise, site and situation affect cities' patterns of growth. Many cities have plentiful space in the cities as well as the surrounding areas, and the concentration of wealth in cities can lead to growth through innovative structures and designs.

Changes that Influence Urbanization

Several factors play an outsized role on urbanization. Transportation and communication innovations have extended urbanization into outlying areas by expediting travel time and increasing cultural interactions. Important inventions in this area include railroads, subways, automobiles, telephones, cell phones, and the Internet. Population growth is a driving force behind urbanization, largely because as the population increases, cities need to expand residential and commercial developments. Migration can further increase population growth as immigrants arrive from rural areas and foreign countries to pursue economic opportunities. Economic development occurs rapidly in urban areas due to the large labor supply and concentration of capital. Finally, government policies can direct and regulate urbanization, especially through the enforcement of zoning laws and building codes.

Cities Across the World

Megacities and Metacities

Spatial factors related to urbanization have led to the creation of **megacities** and **metacities**. The concept of megacities developed in the 1950s to describe cities with populations exceeding 8 million inhabitants. Originally, only New York and London qualified as megacities, but Tokyo joined this exclusive club in the 1960s. Since the 1960s, dozens of megacities have developed all over the world as urbanization has increased. Most recently, human geographers have created the concept of metacities to describe megacities with more sprawling infrastructure. Metacities are relatively unplanned urban

environments spread over a large area of land. In general, metacities have more distinct subsections, dynamic growth patterns, and dramatic demographic shifts than megacities.

Megacities and metacities primarily develop in countries located in the periphery and semi-periphery. Compared to core countries—Canada, the United States, Australia, Japan, and Western Europe—countries located in the periphery and semi-periphery tend to have less economic development and more unstable political systems. However, the non-core countries have industrialized in relatively recent history and enjoyed historically high rates of population growth and urbanization. In 2017, China and India accounted for twenty of the world's forty-seven megacities and metacities. In comparison, the United States and Western Europe combined to account for five megacities and metacities.

Processes of Suburbanization, Sprawl, and Decentralization

Several new land-use models have been created due to the effects of suburbanization, meaning the movement of people and business from core urban centers to outlying areas with lower population density. **Suburbanization** often occurs at an irregular pace with minimal urban planning, resulting in an **urban sprawl** as population density increases across a large area surrounding the city in a sporadic manner. Suburbanization and its sprawling pattern of growth have led to **decentralization** because they transfer economic wealth and political power away from the city's core area. Consequently, new land-use forms have developed in the area's surrounding cities, such as boomburbs, edge cities, and exurbs. **Boomburbs** are suburban areas with rapid rates of population growth, but they retain suburban characteristics, such as smaller buildings and purely residential neighborhoods. **Edge cities** are economic hubs located outside of the city's primary business district. Oftentimes, boomburbs develop around an edge city. **Exurbs** have lower population density than boomburbs, and they feature a mixture of suburban and rural development patterns. The lack of centralized planning in suburbanization and other new land-use forms has presented challenges, such as the depletion of resources from the urban core, traffic congestion, inefficient delivery of services, and pollution.

Cities and Globalization

High population density ensures the rapid spread of new ideas, beliefs, and innovations within urban environments. As such, cities have historically provided the foundation for cultural and artistic movements to flourish. Similarly, cities have historically been important sources of interregional contact due to their heightened role in trade and international economic activities. Combined with the massive trend toward globalized urbanization in the latter half of the twentieth century, the fall of the Soviet Union in 1991 resulted in an expansion of global free trade, strengthening ties between world cities. For example, world cities often serve as the headquarters for international trade groups, multinational corporations, and global financial institutions. Digital technologies have only served to further tighten the economic and cultural connections between cities.

World Cities

Globalization is driven by complex financial relationships and cultural interactions that mostly take place in cities. On a global scale, cities are arranged in an urban hierarchy. World cities lie at the top of the urban hierarchy in both domestic and foreign affairs. Given their large population and consolidation of wealth into a relatively small area, world cities function as the engine for national economies. Similarly, world cities have deep economic and cultural ties to world cities located all over the world. Consequently, the economic and cultural relationships between world cities transmit globalization to the local level due to the importance of the world cities in their home countries.

<u>How Cities are Connected</u>

Cities play roles in a variety of global networks, which is why urban environments mediate processes related to globalization. World cities are almost always the preferred location for businesses involved in international financial services and multinational operations. Some world cities, such as New York and London, also have large-scale stock exchanges with heavy international participation. Other world cities have headquarters for communication and media companies with an international reach, such as San Francisco and Shanghai. Although smaller cities often have some of these international characteristics, world cities are much more likely to be the foundation for multiple global networks.

Cities also tend to have a disproportionately higher rate of immigrants and foreign migrants compared to rural areas. Economic employment and social linkages across immigrant enclaves attract more immigrants, creating a globalized social community that can stretch across continents. At times, international political movements have been able to stage coordinated protests in multiple world cities, such as the Carnival Against Capital (J18 protests) that was held in forty world cities on June 18, 1999.

Size and Distribution of Cities

Geographers apply urban concepts to study cities' distribution, relative size, and relationships to other cities. Hierarchy refers to the ordering of cities based on relative size to emphasize patterns of interdependence. Economic production and relative population size are the most important characteristics in the hierarchical ranking of cities. Often, the hierarchy of cites influences the distribution of cities. For example, the presence of a powerful city might discourage the establishment of smaller cities within the immediate geographic area.

Several principles have been introduced to explain the distribution and size of cities. The **rank-size rule** states that there should be more small cities than large cities. Additionally, it stipulates that large cities effectively consolidate total control over the surrounding area. Geographers also identify primate cities in urban hierarchies. **Primate cities** represent outliers in the urban hierarchy, meaning they have significantly larger populations and societal influence than other large cities. This theory can be used with regional or global scales. For example, New York is a primate city in the northeastern United States, but it's not considered a national primate city. Christaller's **central place theory** asserts that settlements exist primarily to distribute services; therefore, overlapping settlements are more likely to have a triangular or hexagonal pattern to eliminate gaps in distribution.

Internal Structure of Cities

Multiple models and theories have been designed to explain the internal structures of cities. The **Burgess concentric zone** model arranges internal structures based on concentric zones, with the central business district (CBD) functioning as the center. From smallest to largest, the other concentric zones are the transition zone from commercial to residential, working class residential zone, middle-class residential zone, and commuter zone. The **Hoyt sector model** uses the same zones as the Burgess version, but the zones are represented as rectangular sectors growing away from the CBD, which remains at the center. The **Harris and Ullman multiple-nuclei model** asserts that the CBD is not the only center of production, resulting in a more complex representation of internal structures with overlapping and competing zones. The galactic city model represents zones as distinct patterns that flow together, like stars in a constellation. The **bid-rent theory** states that land's potential profitability will dictate land usage within a free market. For example, the theory believes businesses and luxury real estate will be established at the most desirable location. Urban models in Latin America, Southeast Asia, and Africa explore the extreme income inequality between the various zones. In developing countries, high-income

housing and squatter settlements are even more distinct and impenetrable internal structures than in developed countries.

Density and Land Use

Population density reveals distinct patterns of residential land use. **Low-density housing** is exceedingly rare in contemporary urban landscapes. In contrast, low-density housing is most often located in commuter zones. If low-density housing exists near the urban core, the land is likely hazardous or owned by the economic elite. **Medium-density housing** is the most common type of housing in middle-class residential zones. Walk-up apartment buildings are the classic example of medium-population housing. **High-density housing** features large residential buildings, such as high-rise apartment buildings. Squatter settlements can also function as extraordinarily high-density housing.

Residential buildings and land use reflect urban characteristics, such as culture, technology, economic development, and infilling. Culture can influence land use in many ways, ranging from a preference for open spaces to racial redlining. However, land use can also produce cultural changes, such as the tightening of community bonds in mixed land-use developments. Likewise, residential buildings and land-use patterns can reflect technological capabilities. For example, skyscrapers illustrate a society's ability to address overcrowding through advanced vertical construction. Finally, land-use activities often mirror the cities' cycles of development. For example, many cities are engaged in urban renewal and land remediation projects. The transformation of unused or underutilized space into productive areas is commonly referred to as **infilling**.

Infrastructure

Infrastructure is a reflection of cities' political preferences, societal attitudes, and relationship to the environment. The location and quality of infrastructure is a hot-button issue in many cities. Specifically, a lack of access to and underfunding of public transportation is a major concern for low-income communities. Furthermore, cities sometimes build infrastructure to benefit wealthy communities and political allies at the expense of marginalized groups. For example, freeways to suburbs are regularly built through cities' most impoverished communities due to the lower price of land. In addition, wealthy communities typically enjoy disproportionate representation in democratic governments because they're better able to leverage economic resources to gain political capital. A city's emphasis on walkability and public transportation options reflects its commitment to reducing carbon emissions and improving air quality. Cities have faced mounting pressure to sustainable land-use practices and green energy sources as the threat of climate change grows. Public transportation is inarguably the most environmentally sustainable form of transportation due to its efficiency in transporting massive numbers of people. Societal characteristics can also be studied through the amount and type of public spaces. For example, some cities have large public parks and open cultural spaces to stimulate more social interactions.

Urban Sustainability

Cities have implemented several different types of urban design initiatives and zoning practices to limit pollution and increase sustainability. **Mixed land-use development projects** integrate multiple types of zoning practices within the same complex or neighborhood. For example, a mixed-use development project might include commercial, cultural, governmental, and residential units or buildings. **Walkability** initiatives expand inhabitants' ability to travel the city on foot. Among other benefits, walkability initiatives have proven to produce less carbon emissions, more efficient land-use activities, and healthier populations. Examples of walkability initiatives include expanding sidewalks, providing pedestrians with the right-of-way, and excluding vehicles from thoroughfares. **Transportation-oriented development** seeks to maximize the commercial, entertainment, and residential space near public transportation infrastructure.

Smart-growth policies are another class of sustainable design initiatives. **New Urbanism** prioritizes walkability, open spaces, efficient land-use practices, and a strong mixture of housing and employment options. **Greenbelts** are zoning practices intended to protect agricultural land and wilderness from urban development. The most common type of greenbelt is an **urban growth boundary**, which surrounds a city to mark its maximum possible size. **Slow-growth initiatives** seek to reduce sprawl by prioritizing remediation projects, vertical construction, and other projects to avoid expanding the cities' geographic footprint.

Modern urban design initiatives and practices have been widely praised and criticized. Positive effects mostly relate to the practices' environmental and quality-of-life benefits. **Design initiatives** have reduced sprawl by better integrating suburbs with the urban core through public transportation networks, regional planning, and sustainable agricultural production. Other environmental benefits include how modern design initiatives emphasize walkability. Quality of life is improved through zoning practices intended to maintain a supply of affordable housing. More generally, modern urban design practices effectively thwart urban blight and reduce crime, resulting in greater livability.

Negative effects of modern initiatives include price increases and cultural erosion. Although modern urban projects usually include inclusionary zoning practices, the supply of affordable housing almost always falls short of the demand for such housing. This is a natural result of urban renewal projects. As neighborhoods become more desirable, property values rise and rent increases. Further exacerbating this issue, economic revitalization incentivizes real estate developers to invest in upscale luxury apartments. As such, the supply of luxury housing tends to outpace affordable housing as neighborhoods develop. Furthermore, the transformation of urban spaces can change neighborhoods' character. The displacement of local populations through gentrification sometimes results in de facto segregation and the destruction of historical and cultural landmarks.

Urban Data

Geographers collect qualitative and quantitative data to better understand geographic changes within urban environments. Qualitative data is used to construct a written narrative, whereas quantitative data is used in statistical analyses. Overall, qualitative data more effectively reflects nuance and conceptual complexity compared to quantitative data. On the other hand, qualitative data is much more susceptible to overt and subconscious bias because the researchers retain some degree of control over the studies' themes and conclusions. Governments and businesses use qualitative and quantitative data to recognize patterns, diagnose root causes, evaluate ongoing effects, and project future trends. For example, qualitative and quantitative data are both regularly used to optimize land-use activities.

Quantitative Data
Quantitative data plays a critical role in evaluating prospective population growth, demographic changes, and land-use activities. This data is compiled in several ways. Governments collect census data at regular intervals to measure population size, population growth, and demographic trends. For example, the U.S. federal government conducts a census once every ten years. Aside from its application to representative government, census data allows businesses and governments to predict future demand for products and services, including housing and social programs. Businesses generally support

tailoring the census in such a way that it incentivizes the participation of undocumented immigrants. If these groups aren't counted, projections will not accurately reflect true demand. In addition to census data, governments and businesses also conduct more informal surveys about urban changes. Data collection methods for surveys include face-to-face, mail, web, and telephone. However, surveys don't have the same scope and legal weight as a census. As such, surveys must have an appropriate sample size to avoid issues related to false reporting and other discrepancies.

Qualitative Data

Qualitative data analyzes how inhabitants subjectively view urban changes, ranging from broad quality-of-life descriptions to attitudes toward specific trends. In general, text functions as data in qualitative research. Collection of qualitative data can be done through surveys with questions allowing for narrative or long-form responses. In contrast, quantitative data surveys ask all participants the same questions with standardized answer choices, which facilitates statistical analysis. Field studies are another common method of qualitative data collection. Researchers personally enter and interact with the urban environment to conduct field studies. Along with observations, researchers often rely on interviews from inhabitants to form narratives, and the finished report includes descriptive depictions about the urban areas.

Challenges of Urban Changes

Geographic changes to urban areas have economic, political, and social causes. When economic blight persists, it can destroy social networks, create squatter settlements, and result in zones of abandonment. Although urban renewal projects can raise the standard of living in low-income communities, it can cause the rent to skyrocket. As such, municipal governments must strike a fine balance between stimulating economic growth and exacerbating issues related to income inequality.

Economic and Social Challenges

Urban population growth engenders vast socioeconomic challenges. The affordability of rent is among the biggest issue for urban inhabitants. Over the last several decades, urban rent increases have exceeded salary increases in most developed and developing countries. Racial discrimination can also severely disrupt urban housing markets. **Redlining** refers to property owners refusing to sell or rent to certain groups, such as racial minorities. **Blockbusting** is a related concept, and it involves real estate developers using race to scare property owners into selling their houses at below market value.

Given cities' incredible population density, municipal administrations often struggle to efficiently deliver government services. Low-income communities also tend to receive disproportionately less access to services, and they are statistically more likely to suffer from acts of environmental injustice, such as the intentional dumping of pollutants in poor neighborhoods. Rising crime, or the perception of it, can also destabilize social communities and undermine urban economies. **Disamenity zones** occur when the government stops delivering government services to low-income communities, such as in squatter settlements. **Zones of abandonment** arise when crime, poverty, and/or environmental pollution force residents and businesses to flee the area.

Squatter Settlements and Conflicts

Conflicts regularly arise between squatter settlements and municipal administrations. **Squatting** is the unlawful use of land for residential purposes, and the overwhelming majority of squatters are impoverished and/or marginalized in society. Additionally, many squatters reject municipal land tenure schemes, meaning how land is bought, owned, and sold. For example, some squatters believe their settlements accrue some degree of property rights after the passage of time. Municipal administrations rarely side with squatter settlements; instead, they're generally targeted for removal as a quality-of-life issue as well as an economic blight.

Inclusionary Zoning and Local Food Movements

Cities have implemented inclusionary zones and supported local food movements to address urban economic and social challenges. **Inclusionary zoning** involves the changing of city ordinances to mandate a specified amount of affordable housing be built during development projects. Most cities include a range of housing options when implementing inclusionary zoning. For example, a city might require a housing development to institute price controls or offer subsidized units to low-income families. Another major challenge in urban environments is a lack of access to food. **Local food movements** have sought to connect local food producers with urban consumers. Many of these programs promote food produced within the city as a way to increase urban employment or increase environmental sustainability.

Urban Renewal and Gentrification

Municipal administrations must balance urban renewal and gentrification to avoid a socioeconomic crisis. **Urban renewal** includes programs to remove squatter settlements, raise property values, and stimulate economic development. Generally, municipal authorizes will seize land for a development project through eminent domain, meaning the seizure of private property by the government for public use. Most jurisdictions require the government to pay property owners fair market value. Once the land is secured, municipal authorities contract with developers to carry out specific projects. If urban renewal projects are successful, they can raise prices to a point where low-income families cannot afford to remain in the area. This process is known as **gentrification**. Although gentrification generally coincides with periods of economic prosperity, it can dramatically alter communities as affluent residents displace low-income locals.

Functional and Geographic Fragmentation of Governments

Functional and geographic fragmentation of municipal government is a major obstacle to addressing urban challenges. **Functional fragmentation** occurs due to the delegation of municipal authority to multiple agencies operating at different levels of government. For example, housing issues can involve national, state, regional, county, city, and neighborhood governments. At times, these governments might serve competing interests and work to block each other. **Geographic fragmentation** can also frustrate the democratic process and delivery of government services in the urban environment. For example, working with public officials can be difficult for low-income populations when the relevant offices and buildings are spread all across the city.

Challenges of Urban Sustainability

Cities have sought to increase **urban sustainability** in order to avoid depleting natural resources and triggering environmental crises. Urban sustainability has increased in recent years due to the development of green energy sources, which reduces carbon emissions that drive climate change. Other effective sustainability initiatives include investments into public transportation, increased regional planning to optimize land-use strategies, and environmental protection of farmland and wilderness.

Challenges to Urban Sustainability

Urban sustainability faces serious issues caused by rapid population growth and high population density. Overall, cities have a larger ecological footprint than rural areas due to the sheer number of people and their unsustainable consumption of natural resources. **Suburban sprawl** occurs as urbanization spreads

to outlying areas. A lack of public transportation is a major contributing factor in suburban sprawl. Freeways connect suburbs to the urban core, but they also disrupt land-use patterns and increase pollution. Industrial production and residential energy consumption further pollute cities' air and water. Furthermore, urban economic production and energy consumption is a leading cause of climate change, which has resulted in more devastating natural disasters and water shortages. Poor sanitation systems can further degrade the quality of water, and waste disposal is always a high priority for municipal administrations.

Responses to Urban Sustainability Challenges

Municipal administrations have implemented an array of policies to protect the environment and promote urban sustainability. Regional planning efforts support more efficient land-use activities, such as transportation hubs, industrial parks, and farmland protection. The protection of farmland is especially critical because it provides local access to food. Cities sometimes construct urban growth boundaries to protect farmland and natural ecosystems. Under this policy, the boundary line marks the outer limit for urban development. Municipal administrations also actively remediate and redevelop brownfields—areas that have fallen out of use since being developed. Remediation policies typically require cleaning up hazardous waste, whereas redevelopment involves a capital investment into the community.

Practice Questions

Questions 1–3 refer to the diagram below.

Internal Structures of a City

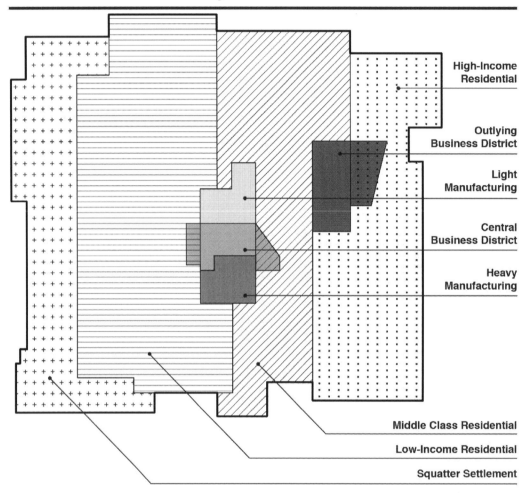

1. Which of the following urban development models is represented in the diagram?
    a. Burgess concentric zone model
    b. Galactic city model
    c. Harris and Ullman multiple-nuclei model
    d. Hoyt sector model
    e. Von Thünen model

2. Compared to the "High-Income Residential" section in the diagram, the "Low-Income Residential" section most likely features which of the following characteristics?
    a. The "Low-Income Residential" section likely has inferior access to critical infrastructure.
    b. The "Low-Income Residential" section likely has a lower population density.
    c. The "Low-Income Residential" section likely has more affordable housing options.
    d. The "Low-Income Residential" section likely has a smaller ecological footprint.
    e. The "Low-Income Residential" section likely has greater access to government agencies.

3. Which of the following most accurately describes the role of "Squatter Settlements" in urban development?
   a. "Squatter Settlements" offer affordable and sustainable housing to marginalized groups.
   b. "Squatter Settlements" pose a quality-of-life issue, although they're generally compliant with municipal land tenure schemes.
   c. "Squatter Settlements" incentivize businesses to invest in the surrounding neighborhood due to the heavy concentration of potential consumers.
   d. "Squatter Settlements" are often included in contemporary inclusionary zoning practices.
   e. "Squatter Settlements" decrease property values, creating a conflict with municipal administrations.

4. Which of the following best explains the difference between site and situation?
   a. Site refers to where developers actively construct buildings, and situation is a commercial development's potential for growth.
   b. Site is a physical location, and situation refers to the location's relationship to surrounding areas.
   c. Site consists of the urban core, and situation encompasses the entire metropolitan region.
   d. Site is the primary focus of socioeconomic systems, and situation exists independently from these systems.
   e. Site only refers to a city's relationship with natural features, and situation covers both man-made and natural features.

Questions 5 and 6 refer to the map below.

Urban Populations in the Northeastern United States (2017)

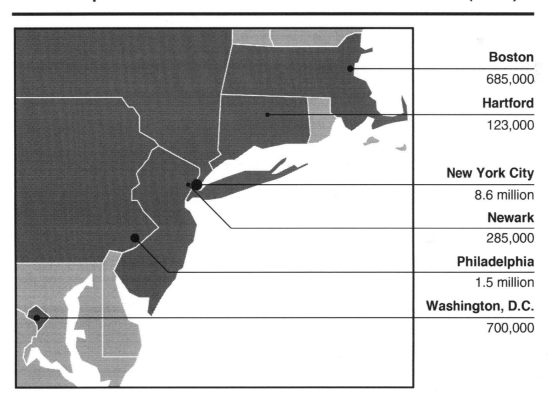

5. Based on the map, New York City is most likely which of the following types of cities?
   a. Edge city
   b. Exurb city
   c. Gravity city
   d. Primate city
   e. Slow-growth city

6. According to the gravity model, which of the following pairs of cities will likely have the most migration interactions?
   a. Boston and Hartford
   b. Hartford and Philadelphia
   c. New York City and Newark
   d. Newark and Philadelphia
   e. Philadelphia and Washington, D.C.

7. Which of the following best describes the motivations for redlining neighborhoods?
   a. Redlining is concerned with preserving a neighborhood's cultural and historical landmarks.
   b. Redlining is motivated by a desire to avoid gentrification.
   c. Redlining is used by real estate developers to scare property owners into selling their homes.
   d. Redlining is used to protect farmland and wilderness areas from urbanization.
   e. Redlining has racial and/or economic motivations.

Question 8 refers to the map below.

Urban Population Density Map

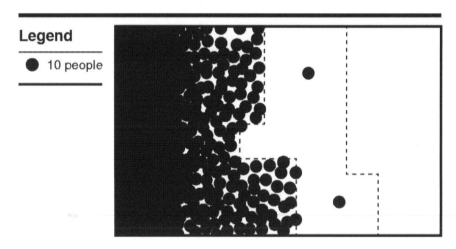

Legend

● 10 people

8. The city's border is most likely based on which of the following urban design practices?
   a. Greenbelt
   b. Inclusionary zoning
   c. Remediation of brownfields
   d. Transportation-oriented development
   e. Vertical construction

9. Which of the following is NOT a concept related to urban sustainability?
    a. Farmland protections
    b. Regional planning efforts
    c. Suburbanization
    d. Transportation-oriented development
    e. Walkability

Question 10 refers to the photograph below.

Residential Buildings in Cleveland (1973)

10. The buildings in the photograph most likely share which of the following characteristics?
    a. Greenbelts
    b. Low population density
    c. Medium population density
    d. High population density
    e. Sprawl

11. An abandoned coal plant turned into a mixed-use land development, a polluted waterfront returned to its natural state of beauty, and industrial waste was removed from an abandoned manufacturing plant. Which of the following best describes these urban land-use projects?
    a. Blockbusting
    b. Brownfield remediation
    c. New Urbanism
    d. Slow-growth initiative
    e. Zones of abandonment

Questions 12–14 refer to the graph below.

Average Housing Prices on Main Street

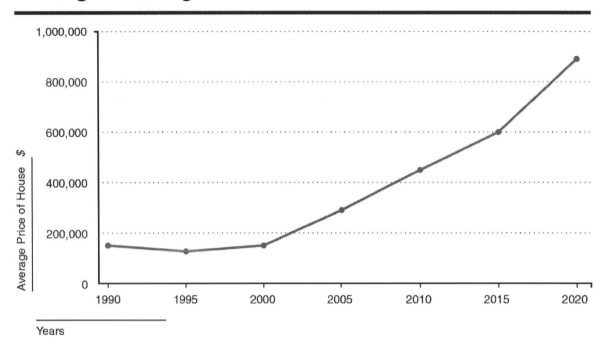

12. The graph is most likely expressing which of the following trends?
    a. Disamenity zones
    b. Gentrification
    c. Geographic fragmentation of government
    d. Slow-growth initiatives
    e. Suburban sprawl

13. Which of the following most likely occurred between 2000 and 2005?
    a. The municipal administration outlawed redlining practices.
    b. The municipal administration condemned several buildings on Main Street.
    c. The municipal administration established an urban growth boundary.
    d. The municipal administration invested in the city's public utilities.
    e. The municipal administration launched a successful urban renewal program.

14. If the municipal administration wanted to address this trend, which of the following actions might they take?
    a. The municipal administration might implement an inclusionary zoning scheme.
    b. The municipal administration might prohibit the practice of blockbusting.
    c. The municipal administration might implement a greenbelt to reduce sprawl.
    d. The municipal administration might subsidize more mixed land-use developments.
    e. The municipal administration might takes steps to reduce geographic fragmentation of government.

15. Which of the following types of suburbanization has relatively low population density and regularly incorporates rural land-use characteristics?

    a. Boomburbs

    b. Decentralized suburbanization

    c. Edge cities

    d. Exurbs

    e. Metacities

Answer Explanations

1. C: The diagram features two different business districts, three residential areas, and a squatter settlement. Both business districts have overlapping residential areas on their right and left. This is similar to the Harris and Ullman multiple-nuclei model, which features multiple centers of production and overlapping areas to express the complexity of internal structures. Choice A is incorrect because the Burgess concentric zone model places different sectors in concentric circles with a central business district at the center. Choice B is incorrect because the galactic city model illustrates internal structures and different cities in a constellation-like pattern to express the fluidity of urban environments. Choice D is incorrect because the Hoyt sector model looks like the Burgess concentric zone model except the sectors are rectangular. Choice E is incorrect because the von Thünen model expresses the arrangement of economic sectors in outlying areas, and it also places the sectors in concentric circles.

2. A: The "Low-Income Residential" section is located between the "Squatter Settlement" and "Central Business District." Within urban environments, low-income residential areas typically have inferior access to critical infrastructure. Municipal administrations commit more resources to middle-class and high-income communities due to their disproportionate political influence compared to low-income communities. Choice B is incorrect because low-income residential areas often have a higher population density due to their inhabitants having fewer resources to secure extra space in housing. Choice C is incorrect because there are a lack of affordable housing options in most contemporary cities. Additionally, middle-class and high-income families usually have more affordable housing options due to their greater resources. Choice D is incorrect because low-income residential areas generally have a higher ecological footprint due to their greater population density. Choice E is incorrect because although some government agencies might be located in low-income residential areas, these agencies are typically spread across the city. Additionally, proximity to the agencies doesn't necessarily translate to greater access.

3. E: "Squatter Settlements" appear on the far left of the diagram, bordering the "Low-Income Residential" area. Squatter settlements often develop in this type of location due to squatters being pushed to the margins of society because they can't afford low-income housing. Municipal administrations often target squatter settlements for removal because these settlements can cause economic blight, which decreases property values. Choice A is incorrect because squatter settlements cannot be reasonably characterized as sustainable housing; squatters generally live in makeshift housing and face serious sanitation challenges. Choice B is incorrect because although squatter settlements can pose a quality-of-life issue, they're almost never compliant with municipal land tenure schemes, which govern how land is bought, owned, and sold. Cities rarely extend property rights to squatters. Choice C is incorrect due to squatter settlements discouraging investment because they pose sanitation and safety issues. Choice D is incorrect because inclusionary zoning practices require affordable housing units to be included in new development projects. Often, inclusionary zoning practices are implemented in an effort to eliminate squatter settlements.

4. B: Site is a city's physical location. As such, site influences the origin, function, and growth of cities based on geographic position and climatic conditions. Situation is a related concept, but it involves the city's relationship to surrounding areas, which includes man-made and natural features. Therefore, the major difference is that site is limited to a city's physical location, and situation is much broader, encompassing relationships to surrounding areas. Choice A is incorrect because although the concepts of site and situation can be applied to development projects, they carry the same meaning as expressed in Choice B. Choice C is incorrect because although situation can encompass an entire metropolitan

area, site is not limited to the urban core. Choice *D* is incorrect because these concepts aren't primarily focused on socioeconomic systems. Choice *E* is incorrect because site refers to physical location, not a relationship with natural features.

5. D: The map expresses how New York City dwarfs other regional cities in terms of population. In fact, New York City's population is nearly six times greater than the next most populous city (Philadelphia). Given this vast discrepancy in population size, it can be inferred that New York City also has a larger economy and more cultural influence than the other cities. This degree of regional dominance is the hallmark of a primate city. Choice *A* is incorrect because edge cities are prosperous economic centers that develop in suburban areas. Choice *B* is incorrect because exurbs are a new suburban land-use form with relatively low population density. Choice *C* is incorrect because gravity is not a type of city; it's a characteristic of a city that describes its ability to attract migrants from nearby cities. Choice *E* is incorrect because although slow-growth cities attempt to reduce suburban sprawl through a variety of initiatives, such as remediation projects and vertical construction, the map doesn't contain enough information to determine whether New York City is a slow-growth city.

6. C: The gravity model describes how large and powerful cities have a stronger pull on nearby cities, especially in terms of attracting migrants. Within the region depicted on this map, New York City would have an extremely strong gravitational pull based on its population size. Because gravitational pull increases based on proximity, New York City would have the most migration interactions with Newark. Choice *A* is incorrect because although Boston has a significantly larger population than Hartford, the chasm between New York City and Newark is much wider. Choice *B* is incorrect because the distance between Hartford and Philadelphia is much greater than the distance between New York City and Newark. Choice *D* is incorrect because Philadelphia is much smaller than New York City and farther away from Newark. Choice *E* is incorrect because although Philadelphia has more than twice the population of Washington, D.C., there's considerable distance between the two cities.

7. E: Redlining is a practice in which a group of property owners jointly refuse to sell or rent housing units to specific groups of people. Racial minorities are by far the most frequent targets of redlining. Property owners and landlords have two primary motivations for redlining—racial prejudice and a fear that racial minorities will trigger a decline in housing prices. Choice *A* is incorrect because although, when combined with racial prejudice, property owners' concern with preserving a neighborhood's cultural and historical landmarks can lead to redlining, Choice *E* more directly states the motivations behind redlining. Choice *B* is incorrect because redlining is not related to gentrification, which refers to how neighborhood demographics change as property values increase. Choice *C* is incorrect because it states the definition of blockbusting. Choice *D* is incorrect because it describes the urban sustainability concept of greenbelt or urban growth boundary.

8. A: The map depicts a city with clearly defined borders. Compared to the sections of the map labeled "Farmland" and "Wilderness," the city has an exponentially higher population density. In other words, there is very limited suburban sprawl. A greenbelt is an urban sustainability initiative that's implemented to protect farmland and wilderness from suburbanization and other sprawling patterns of urban development. Based on the vast differences in population density, the city likely established a greenbelt. Choice *B* is incorrect because inclusionary zoning practices theoretically increase the supply of affordable housing by forcing developers to include such units in new residential projects. Choice *C* is incorrect because brownfields are areas that have been abandoned or heavily polluted, and the remediation of brownfields is often included in urban renewal projects. Choice *D* is incorrect because transportation-oriented development refers to the construction of new commercial, entertainment, and residential development projects close to public transportation systems. Choice *E* is incorrect because vertical construction is a slow-growth initiative, and it involves creating more urban space through the construction of taller buildings.

9. C: Suburbanization involves an expansion of residential units and commercial activities outside of the urban core. This can result in a decentralized, sprawling growth pattern, which increases pollution and the consumption of natural resources. Choice *A* is incorrect because urban sustainability initiatives seek to avoid draining natural resources, limit pollution, and increase livability. Farmland protections, such as urban growth boundaries, reduce pollution by promoting the consumption of locally produced food. Choice *B* is incorrect because regional planning increases the efficiency of land-use activities by limiting sprawl. Choice *D* is incorrect because transportation-oriented development decreases pollution by maximizing the effectiveness of public transportation. Likewise, Choice *E* is incorrect because walkability initiatives reduce carbon emissions.

10. D: Based on the information contained in the title, the buildings in the photograph are residential buildings. These are massive structures with approximately twenty floors visible, and given its considerable width, it's reasonable to assume each floor has more than a dozen units. Furthermore, the photograph depicts three of these structures in proximity to each other, so the buildings have high population density. Choice *A* is incorrect because greenbelts are an urban sustainability initiative, and they're primarily implemented to protect farmland and wilderness areas. Choice *B* is incorrect because low population density is more common in rural areas and wealthy suburbs than urban areas. In any event, buildings of this size cannot reasonably be characterized as having low population density. Likewise, Choice *C* is incorrect because walk-up apartment buildings and townhouse complexes are classic examples of medium population density structures; the buildings in the photograph house significantly more people in a smaller geographic area. Choice *E* is incorrect because sprawl is a pattern of growth that's most closely associated with suburbanization.

11. B: The prompt includes three examples of land-use projects. One example involves the redevelopment of an abandoned area, and the other two examples describe the removal of pollutants. Municipal administrations conduct brownfield remediation projects to redevelop abandoned areas and remove pollution from the environment. As such, these examples are brownfield remediation projects. Choice *A* is incorrect because blockbusting is a tactic used by real estate developers, and it involves stoking racial prejudice to reduce real estate prices. Choice *C* is incorrect because New Urbanism refers to a series of smart-growth policies, and these policies emphasize urban sustainability initiatives, such as walkability and mixed-use development projects. Choice *D* is incorrect because slow-growth initiatives emphasize limiting sprawl and reducing the cities' geographic footprint. Choice *E* is incorrect because zones of abandonment have high rates of people migrating out of the area, largely due to rampant crime, systemic poverty, and/or lethal levels of pollution. Some brownfields can be classified as zones of abandonment, but the examples describe the remediation of brownfields.

12. B: The graph depicts skyrocketing housing prices on Main Street. Between 2000 and 2020, housing prices more than quintupled. Gentrification typically coincides with rapidly increasing housing prices. Choice *A* is incorrect because disamenity zones are areas where the government cannot or will not deliver services. Property prices are increasing on Main Street, so there's no reason for the government to stop delivering services. Choice *C* is incorrect because geographic fragmentation of government can reduce access to public officials and government services, especially for low-income populations; the data doesn't indicate that there's a geographic fragmentation of government in this area. Choice *D* is incorrect because slow-growth initiatives increase urban sustainability, and they don't directly relate to housing price increases. Likewise, Choice *E* is incorrect because suburban sprawl is a decentralized pattern of urban growth, which cannot explain this trend by itself.

13. E: The price of housing on Main Street nearly doubled between 2000 and 2005. Urban renewal projects target sources of economic blight and pollution for removal. If successful, urban renewal projects can cause property values to increase in the surrounding areas, which could lead to gentrification. Choice A is incorrect because although a prohibition on redlining could increase the demand for housing, it couldn't reasonably result in such a sharp increase in price. Choice B is incorrect because if the municipal administration condemned buildings on Main Street, it could potentially result in a greater supply of housing. Theoretically, this would decrease housing prices. In any event, it couldn't explain the price of housing doubling. Choice C is incorrect because urban growth boundaries limit sprawl and protect outlying areas from economic development, which isn't directly related to property values. Choice D is incorrect because an investment in public utilities would only result in a marginal increase to housing prices.

14. A: If the municipal administration wanted to address the skyrocketing housing prices, they would seek to increase the supply of affordable housing. An inclusionary zoning scheme could accomplish this goal because it would force developers to include affordable units in new residential development projects. Choice B is incorrect because although blockbusting is a nefarious practice used by real estate developers to artificially lower housing prices, a prohibition on blockbusting wouldn't effectively address this crisis. Choice C is incorrect because implementing a greenbelt would reduce sprawl, but it wouldn't address the skyrocketing housing prices. Choice D is incorrect because mixed land-use practices integrate commercial, cultural, government, and residential units in development projects. This would address the housing supply; however, inclusionary zoning is more closely related to increasing the affordable housing supply. Choice E is incorrect because although geographic fragmentation of government is an urban political challenge, it's not directly related to the housing supply.

15. D: Exurbs combine suburban and rural settlement patterns. As such, exurbs have lower population density than most suburban areas. In addition, exurbs tend to have rural land-use characteristics, such as open spaces and agricultural production. Choice A is incorrect because boomburbs have high rates of population growth, resulting in higher than average population density compared to other suburban areas. Choice B is incorrect because although decentralized suburbanization can result in relatively low population density, it's not commonly associated with rural land-use characteristics. Choice C is incorrect because edge cities are prosperous economic centers that develop outside of the urban core, and they often result in the growth of boomburbs. Choice E is incorrect because metacities are megacities with sprawling infrastructure and staggeringly high population density.

Industrial and Economic Development Patterns and Processes

Industrial Revolution

While Europe was in the midst of colonization and revolutions, they experienced an **industrial revolution** that would impact the social and economic fabric of life. Starting in the 1760s, with humble origins in England's textile economy, it lasted until the 1820s and changed the way people worked and lived. The revolution brought new scientific developments and improvements to agriculture and textile manufacturing. It was also a time of great invention in steam- and water-powered engines, machines, tools, chemicals, transportation, factories, lighting, glass, cement, medicines, and many more. Additional information concerning the Industrial Revolution and the Second Industrial Revolution are included in the section called "The Major Economic Transformations that Have Affected World Societies."

In some ways, the Industrial Revolution improved people's standard of living, but in many ways, it made life harder. Falling prices on goods made nutrition levels improve and allowed people more buying power. Medicines and better transportation also improved the quality of life for many. However, crowded living quarters in the booming urban centers were often appalling, as were the diseases brought on by working in factory conditions. The use of child labor eventually brought about reform, and labor unions had an effect on working conditions, but it took many years for either of these problems to be addressed.

Economic Sectors and Patterns

Industrial production and development creates distinct spatial patterns. Economic activity requires a significant amount of resources and space, and countries regularly place similar types of economic production in the same area to increase efficiency. Spatial patterns illustrate concentration of economic activity; therefore, different economic sectors can be easily identified in visual representations.

Different Economic Sectors

Economic sectors have five different patterns of development: primary, secondary, tertiary, quaternary, and quinary. All of these patterns are distinct, allowing economic activities and trends to be identified based on recognition of pattern. The **primary economic sector** creates development patterns based on the extraction of raw resources, such as agricultural products, minerals, and fossil fuels. These development patterns cover vast distances and release significant amounts of pollutants into the natural environment. The **secondary economic sector** mostly involves manufacturing, and this activity creates concentrated patterns of intense development. The **tertiary economic sector** is the service industry, including transportation, hospitality, and restaurant staff. This sector is typically the largest by a considerable margin. The **quaternary economic sector** is service jobs within the knowledge economy, including accounting, communication, legal, and research jobs. The quaternary economic sector is a critical aspect of development in advanced industrial economies, particularly in its connection to globalization. The **quinary economic sector** is the smallest by far, consisting of an elite group of executives with decision-making powers. Consequently, the quinary economic sector sits atop the urban hierarchy and influences the trajectory of globalized patterns of development.

<u>Break-of-Bulk Point, Least Cost Theory, Labor, Transportation, Markets, and Resources</u>
Manufacturers decide whether to locate plants in core, semi-periphery, and periphery locations based on many factors, such as the break-of-bulk point, least cost theory, financial costs, labor supply, transportation systems, market access, and availability of resources. The **break-of-bulk point** is the location where cargo is transferred from one transportation system to another. For example, a break-of-bulk point occurs at seaports where ships' cargo is loaded onto trucks to be transported. **Manufacturing centers** tend to develop in the immediate area surrounding the break-of-bulk point due to the **least cost theory**, which states that businesses seek to minimize financial costs, such as labor and transportation. **Labor supply** has a strong impact on labor costs of manufacturing. For example, if the supply of labor exceeds demand, labor costs will decline, attracting manufacturing plants. **Transportation systems** increase market access and the availability of resources for manufacturing, so businesses seek to locate their plants near transportation systems to limit the financial costs of production.

Measures of Development

Measures of Social and Economic Development
The most common tool for measuring economic growth is the **Gross Domestic Product (GDP)**. The increase of goods and services over time indicates positive movement in economic growth. The quantity of goods and services produced is not always an indicator of economic growth, however; the value of the goods and services produced matters more than the quantity.

There are many causes of economic growth, which can be short- or long-term. In the short term, if aggregate demand (the total demand for goods and services produced at a given time) increases, then the overall GDP increases as well. As the GDP increases, interest rates may decrease, which may encourage greater spending and investing. Real estate prices may also rise, and there may be lower income taxes. All of these short-term factors can stimulate economic growth.

In the long term, if aggregate supply (the total supply of goods or services in a given time period) increases, then there is potential for an increase in capital as well. With more working capital, more infrastructure and jobs can be created. With more jobs, there is an increased employment rate, and education and training for jobs will improve. New technologies will be developed, and new raw materials may be discovered. All of these long-term factors can also stimulate economic growth.

Other causes of economic growth include low inflation and stability. Lower inflation rates encourage more investing as opposed to higher inflation rates that cause market instability. Stability encourages businesses to continue investing. If the market is unstable, investors may question the volatility of the market.

Potential Costs of Economic Growth:

- **Inflation**: When economic growth occurs, inflation tends to be high. If supply cannot keep up with demand, then the inflation rate may be unmanageable.
- **Economic booms and recessions**: The economy goes through cycles of booms and recessions. This causes inflation to fluctuate over time, which puts the economy into a continuous cycle of rising and falling.
- **Account inefficiencies**: When the economy grows, consumers and businesses increase their import spending. The increase of import spending affects the current account and causes a shortage.

- **Environmental costs**: When the economy is growing, there is an abundance of output, which may result in more pollutants and a reduction in quality of life.
- **Inequalities**: Growth occurs differently among members of society. While the wealthy may be getting richer, those living in poverty may just be getting on their feet. So, while economic growth is happening, it may happen at very different rates.

While these potential costs could affect economic growth, if the growth is consistent and stable, then it can occur without severe inflation swings. As technology improves, new ways of production can reduce negative environmental factors as well.

Measures of Gender Inequality

The United Nations Development Programme (UNDP) introduced the **Gender Inequality Index (GII)** in 2010 for the purpose of more accurately ranking gender inequality. Previously, the UNDP had used the Gender Development Index (GDI) and Gender Empowerment Measure (GEM), but critics challenged these measures' efficacy based on their emphasis on economic development and income levels. Often, the reliance on economic factors meant that GDI and GEM rankings would be strikingly similar to the Human Development Index (HDI) regardless of whether a country suffered deeply rooted gender inequality. In effect, the similar rankings created an incorrect implication that gender inequality wasn't relevant to human and economic development. The GII improved the measurement of gender inequality by concentrating on three dimensions—reproductive health, female empowerment, and labor market participation for women. In addition, all three dimensions are measured independent of each other, which prevents success in one dimension from completely counterbalancing failures in another dimension.

Because none of these measures are directly tied to economic development, the GII specifically reflects levels of gender inequality. For example, a developing country with minimal gender inequality could outperform an advanced industrial country on the GII. This would have been impossible with the previous measures.

Human Development Index (HDI)

Mahbub ul Haq, a Pakistani economist, developed the **Human Development Index (HDI)** for the United Nations Development Programme (UNDP). The HDI seeks to rank countries based on their performance in three key measures: life expectancy at birth, mean and expected years of educational achievement, and per capita income. Ul Haq intended the HDI to reflect his theories of human development, which prioritizes the freedoms of "being" and doing." The freedom of "being" encompasses being sheltered and physically nurtured, and the freedom of "doing" includes the right to vote, pursue employment opportunities, and interact with the community.

In contrast to previous measures of development, the HDI emphasizes both economic and quality-of-life factors. Most recently, the UNDP developed the **Inequality-adjusted Human Development Index (IHDI)** to reflect how inequality can undermine a population from reaching its potential capacity for development. However, the IHDI has been criticized for ignoring a country's wealth per capita and relative quality of economic products. As a result, some highly developed countries tend to perform worse on the IHDI. For example, in 2014, the United States ranked fifth in HDI but twenty-eighth in IHDI due to the country's lack of success in developing its poorest communities compared to other highly developed countries.

Women and Economic Development

Economic development has generally improved gender parity since the 1950s. Prior to this period, the United Nations and international organizations focused simply on spurring economic development and increasing standard of living. International aid was intended to fight inflation, reduce unemployment, expand professional opportunities, and subsidize programs to provide basic services such as affordable housing and health care. However, a singular focus on economic development didn't address the marginalization of women. In response, recent programs have sought to directly incorporate women into economic development, which has resulted in more professional, educational, and leadership opportunities for women.

Changing Roles of Women

The **socioeconomic roles of women** differ across regions, and these roles are dynamic, transforming during the various stages of economic development. In most developing countries, women serve a dual role as traditional homemakers and an agricultural labor source. Agriculture in developing countries tends to be unorganized and more ad hoc than other economic sectors, such as real estate, trade, and finance. Because women are often denied entry into other economic sectors due to educational barriers and household responsibilities, they overwhelmingly concentrate on agriculture, fishing, and hunting to feed their families. In some African countries, women account for up to 80 percent of agricultural workers.

When the United Nations initially promulgated economic development programs, it failed to take into account the roles women played in local economies. Financial loans would primarily be to male-dominated economic sectors. In addition, women received minimal voice in how countries developed agriculturally, even if they dominated the actual workforce. This led to considerable inefficiencies. International efforts to implement a gender-informed economic development have been relatively successful at addressing this issue. Microloans and increased female participation in leadership have allowed more women to join other economic sectors and generally become more financially independent.

Increased Female Workforce Does Not Mean Equity in Wages

Despite increased female workforce participation over the last several decades, especially in the developing world, pervasive gender inequality persists. Women routinely have inferior access to employment opportunities. In the developing world, men continue to dominate political and societal power structures, effectively prohibiting women from serving in a leadership capacity. As a result, women often struggle to transcend their traditional role within the household. A similar problem exists in developed countries, although to a lesser extent. Women continue to be underrepresented in leadership roles in elite professional and governmental bodies. In addition, women generally enjoy less equity in wages. The World Economic Forum introduced the Gender Gap Index (GGI) in 2006 to rank countries based on disparities in income. Overall, countries have sought to address these issues through affirmative action programs, labor regulations, and microloans to support more female entrepreneurism.

Microloans

Microloans refer to a specific type of financial aid to developing countries that are intended to improve standards of living. Men often dominate economic, political, and social power structures, and therefore microloans represent an effort to directly bring women into the development process. Without this type of direct aid, the financial benefits of economic development can exclude women due to their lack of access to educational and professional opportunities. In addition, many experts point to how women are more likely to serve as the heads of households in developed countries. As such, microloans to women can be seen as the most efficient method of raising quality of life for families. However, microloans have been controversial with socialists, environmentalists, and feminists. To varying degrees, these groups criticize microloans for upholding the capitalist status quo and failing to produce structural changes. Compared to wealth redistribution, microloans take significantly longer to address deep-rooted issues. In addition, the use of capitalist policies to address gender issues has raised concerns over unsustainable levels of consumption, pollution, and environmental destruction.

Theories of Development

Rostow's Stages of Economic Growth model argues that development occurs across five linear stages. Stage one is a traditional agricultural society with no centralized government. Stage two is preconditions for an economic takeoff, such as infrastructure and dissemination of technology. Stage three is an economic takeoff driven by industrialization and urbanization. Stage four is countries' transition from developing to developed status. Stage five is characterized by mass production and consumption.

Wallerstein's World System Theory classifies countries as core, semi-periphery, and periphery in a global hierarchy. The **core countries** are the United States, Canada, Western Europe, Australia, and Japan. The **semi-periphery** includes the largest emergent economies, such as India, China, Brazil, and South Africa. The **periphery** consists of developing countries. **Dependency theory** is similar to World System Theory except it argues that periphery countries are impoverished because they function as a source of raw resources and unskilled labor for core countries to exploit. **Commodity dependence** argues that countries struggle to develop when they overly rely on exporting commodities, such as fossil fuels and agricultural products. Dependent countries are typically vulnerable to downturns and lack incentives to pursue development.

Trade and the World Economy

Complementarity and Comparative Advantage

Complementarity and comparative advantage dictate how trade patterns develop. Theoretically, countries seek to import what they don't have and export their surplus. Complementarity refers to when countries are compatible for trading purposes, meaning they can provide exports in exchange for the items they need. For example, a country with a weak industrial sector and strong agricultural sector would seek a complementary trading partner with the inverse situation. Comparative advantage refers to how countries will produce the most goods with the lowest opportunity costs. Countries seek to maximize the benefits of comparative advantage by exporting goods with the lowest opportunity costs and importing goods with the highest opportunity costs for domestic production.

Neoliberal Policies

Neoliberalism is a nebulous term, with its meaning depending on usage, but neoliberal policies generally include austerity, deregulation, free trade, and privatization. This doctrine rapidly spread in the post-Cold War era as capitalism increasingly asserted itself as the only viable economic ideology. Many international organizations have been established to spread neoliberal policies related to free trade. The **World Trade Organization (WTO)** was established in 1995 to create a legal and logistical framework for free-trade deals and provide a dispute resolution forum. Mercosur promotes free trade in South America through establishing a customs union across members' territories and negotiating collective trade policies with foreign powers. The **European Union (EU)** also began as a customs union, but it later integrated politically, becoming a supranational state. The **Organization of the Petroleum**

Exporting Countries (OPEC) was formed to maximize market coordination between nations with large-scale oil production and proven reserves.

Government Initiatives

Government initiatives strongly impact economic development. Countries sometimes introduce tariffs to decrease the competitiveness of exports for the purpose of protecting domestic industries. Many countries seek to develop self-sufficient industries in critical sectors, such as steel and energy. On the other hand, countries adopt free-trade policies to benefit from the rising levels of international trade. Free-trade agreements can also attract foreign investment in development projects. However, these agreements often have clauses preventing countries from implementing stringent labor and environmental protections.

How Different Economies Have Become More Closely Connected

National economies have become increasingly connected and, at times, interdependent. International finance has played a particularly significant role in creating a global marketplace. Capital can flow across borders in an instant, and nearly all countries enjoy large-scale foreign investment. International lending agencies, such as the International Monetary Fund (IMF) and World Bank, also provide massive aid to developing countries if they adopt neoliberal policies. For example, Argentina and Greece have passed austerity measures, such as cuts to social programs and pensions, to qualify for IMF loans. Development strategies also reflect an international commitment to capitalism, such as microlending programs that promote entrepreneurialism rather than wealth redistribution. Economic interdependence is also reflected in global financial crises. For example, the Great Recession began when the U.S. financial sector veered toward collapse in 2007, and the danger quickly spread to closely connected European and South American financial markets. Concern over sovereign debt crises is a major reason the IMF provides loans in exchange for austerity measures.

Changes as a Result of the World Economy

International trade has increased exponentially since the 1980s for a number of reasons, including the collapse of the Soviet Union, creation of the World Trade Organization (WTO), and advent of digital technologies. International trade has led to a more interdependent world economy as countries increasingly rely on trade partners to secure goods, services, and natural resources. In addition, there have been significant geographic consequences as newly established international organizations and supranational governments tie diverse regions together. In the developing world, urbanization and industrialization have rapidly increased as advanced industrial countries embrace deindustrialization, transferring manufacturing and blue-collar jobs overseas.

Outsourcing and Economic Restructuring

Patterns of economic production have shifted dramatically over the last several decades. Businesses in core countries have engaged in **outsourcing**, meaning the transfer of jobs overseas to reduce labor and environmental costs. Outsourcing has primarily impacted manufacturing and other blue-collar jobs, and these jobs are typically relocated to industrializing countries in the periphery and semi-periphery. Outsourcing has resulted in core countries undergoing a process known as **economic restructuring** in which blue-collar jobs are replaced with white-collar service jobs. However, a significant number of blue-collar workers lack the skills and experience to make this transition.

International Division of Labor

The **international division of labor** is a hierarchy with the core countries holding the vast majority of specialized manufacturing and white-collar service jobs. Compared to core countries, countries located in the semi-periphery and periphery have lower levels of compensation. However, there has been significant economic growth in the semi-periphery and periphery. Specifically, several different types of new manufacturing zones have emerged in these regions, and they have been a source of tremendous economic growth. Special economic zones attract foreign manufacturers to relocate and outsource production. Compared to the rest of the developed country, a special economic zone typically has reduced taxes, fewer labor laws, weaker environmental protections, and fewer trade restrictions. Free-trade zones are a type of special economic zone where goods can be imported, stored, manufactured, and/or exported without paying customs duties. Most free-trade zones are located near airports, seaports, and borders. Export processing zones are a type of free-trade zone that specializes in manufacturing products to export.

Contemporary Economic Landscape

The **contemporary economic landscape** has undergone a dramatic transformation due to a multitude of factors. **Post-Fordist methods of production** emphasize flexibility in delivering specialized goods to specifically targeted populations. **Multiplier effects** create a spillover effect in economic activities, such as how buying locally produced goods strengthens the local economy. **Economies of scale** have encouraged businesses to grow and merge because costs decrease as production increases. **Agglomeration** is the physical concentration of businesses, and it spurs commercial growth by reducing transportation costs, increasing access to consumers, and expanding resource pools. **Just-in-time delivery** decreases the amount of time between the production and delivery of goods. The expansion of **service sectors**, such as banking and programming, have created employment opportunities and spurred economic growth with relatively less pollution. **High-technology industries** drive innovation and economic production, especially in advanced industrial economies. **Growth poles** are economic sectors that exceed the national economic growth average, and they can stimulate economic growth, particularly in world cities.

Sustainable Development

Sustainability principles impact industrialization and spatial development in an attempt to limit the harm caused by economic production. Capitalism is predicated on exploiting natural resources for profit and continually increasing levels of consumption. Rather than addressing structural economic issues, sustainability is concerned with reforming industrialization to reduce and/or mitigate environmental harm. In turn, the application of sustainability principles can also alter spatial development, such as preserving wilderness and regulating where industries are located.

Sustainable Development Policies

Sustainable development attempts to balance economic growth with environmental protection. Industrialization and urbanization have devastated ecosystems due to the release of waste products and toxic pollutants into the environment. Additionally, sustainable development is concerned with reducing society's consumption of fossil fuels to limit the harmful effects of climate change. Sustainable energy policies prioritize the development of green energy—solar, wind, and hydropower—and an expansion of public transportation to decrease the number of cars on the road. Additionally, sustainable development encompasses methods of mitigating the harmful impact of climate change, such as the increased frequency of natural disasters and water shortages. Another critical part of sustainable development is limiting the mass consumption of consumer goods. Mass consumption increases

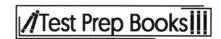

pollution and results in the depletion of natural resources. Although recycling has addressed some of these issues, mass consumption continues to be the norm in much of the world.

Ecotourism

Ecotourism refers to when tourists travel to relatively undisturbed natural locations, such as national parks or forests. Supporters cite several benefits of ecotourism. Revenue from ecotourism helps fund conservation projects to keep the location pristine, and the industry expands employment opportunities for local populations. Additionally, ecotourism is educational for tourists, fostering a greater understanding of and respect for the natural environment and indigenous cultures. However, ecotourism has recently experienced an economic boom with an annual growth rate of more than 10 percent. As ecotourism becomes increasingly popular, it becomes less sustainable and more threatening to the natural environment. A major problem lies in the foreign and corporate ownership of companies engaged in ecotourism. These commercial actors often divert funds from conservation, ignore environmental degradation, provide minimal compensation to local employees, and displace indigenous communities.

The UN's Sustainable Development Goals

The United Nations Development Programme oversees long-term **Sustainable Development Goals (Global Goals)**. These Global Goals are aspirational and intended to measure how development projects are progressing. In 2015, UN member states unanimously adopted seventeen Global Goals to be achieved by 2030. These seventeen goals share a common commitment to social stability, economic development, and environmental sustainability. Furthermore, the goals are integrated, meaning progress toward one goal will have a positive impact on the pursuit of several other goals. Examples of recent goals include ending poverty, sustainable urban development, gender equality, climate action, and protection of all life below water and on land. Policy prescriptions accompany most of these broad Global Goals, such as using small-scale financing and microloan programs to alleviate poverty. Some policy changes can also affect numerous goals by addressing large-scale issues, such as how an expansion of public transportation can lower fossil fuel emissions.

Practice Questions

Question 1 refers to the photograph below.

Old Faithful Geyser in Yellowstone National Park

1. Which of the following involves the commercialization of environmental features similar to the one depicted in the photograph?
   a. Ecotourism
   b. Growth poles
   c. Neoliberalism
   d. Outsourcing
   e. Sustainable development

Questions 2 and 3 refer to the diagram below.

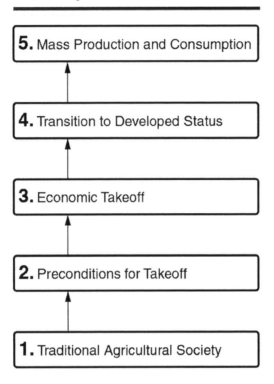

Trajectory of Economic Development

5. Mass Production and Consumption

↑

4. Transition to Developed Status

↑

3. Economic Takeoff

↑

2. Preconditions for Takeoff

↑

1. Traditional Agricultural Society

2. The diagram is based on which of the following theories?
   a. Bid-rent theory
   b. Dependency theory
   c. New Urbanism
   d. Rostow's Stages of Economic Growth
   e. Wallerstein's World Systems Theory

3. Where would Western European countries be plotted on the diagram?
   a. Box 1
   b. Box 2
   c. Box 3
   d. Box 4
   e. Box 5

4. Which of the following is a component of the Human Development Index?
   a. Civil liberties
   b. Environmental sustainability
   c. Female empowerment
   d. Per capita income
   e. Reproductive health

Questions 5 and 6 refer to the map below.

Economic Development of the Americas

Legend

■ Core countries

▨ Semi-periphery countries

■ Periphery countries

5. The map depicts a classification system used in which of the following pairs of theories?
   a. Commodity dependence and dependency theory
   b. Commodity dependence and Wallerstein's World Systems Theory
   c. Dependency theory and Wallerstein's World Systems Theory
   d. Rostow's Stages of Economic Growth and dependency theory
   e. Wallerstein's World Systems Theory and Rostow's Stages of Economic Growth

6. Which of the following most accurately explains the difference between core and periphery countries?

    a. Core countries exclusively specialize in high-technology industries, whereas periphery countries specialize in manufacturing.

    b. Core countries have highly advanced industrial economies with a large service sector, and periphery countries function as a source of cheap labor in the global economic system.

    c. Core countries have significantly larger economies than periphery countries, but periphery countries more equitably distribute wealth among their citizens.

    d. Core countries extract raw resources from periphery countries, whereas periphery countries are the primary beneficiaries of free-trade agreements.

    e. Core countries are located in Western Europe, and periphery countries are mostly found in the Americas and East Asia.

7. Which of the following is NOT a United Nations Development Programme Sustainable Development Goal for 2030?

    a. Climate action

    b. Ending poverty

    c. Gender equality

    d. Preventing gentrification

    e. Sustainable urban development

Questions 8–10 refer to the table below.

Regional Comparison of Adjusted Net Income Per Capita (2017)	
Country	Income Per Capita ($)
East Asia and Pacific	8061
European Union	28,096
Latin America and Caribbean	7784
Middle East and North Africa	6158
North America	50,014
South Asia	1624
Sub-Saharan Africa	1235

Source: The World Bank, 2017

8. Based on the table, which of the following regions likely struggles the most with economic development?

    a. European Union

    b. Latin America and Caribbean

    c. Middle East and North Africa

    d. North America

    e. Sub-Saharan Africa

9. Which of the following best explains why North America has the highest income per capita?
   a. North American countries established numerous special economic zones and export processing zones.
   b. North America has significant amounts of natural resources.
   c. North American countries have forged deep economic ties to the European Union.
   d. North American countries adopted neoliberal economic policies.
   e. North America is the home of two core countries.

10. According to dependency theory, why does South Asia have an extremely low income per capita?
   a. South Asian countries are overly dependent on exporting commodities.
   b. Core countries exploit South Asian countries' natural resources and workforce.
   c. South Asian countries are dependent on subsistence agriculture, undermining the transition to commercial agriculture.
   d. Core countries have outsourced blue-collar manufacturing jobs to South Asia.
   e. South Asian countries rely on ecotourism to gain support from international lending agencies.

11. Which of the following best summarizes how multiplier effects have impacted the contemporary economic landscape?
   a. Multiplier effects facilitate the concentration of businesses, reducing transportation costs and expanding businesses' access to resources.
   b. Multiplier effects provide flexibility in specialized manufacturing.
   c. Multiplier effects spur economic growth through creating a spillover effect in which one economic activity benefits several other activities.
   d. Multiplier effects have created the regulatory framework for international trade.
   e. Multiplier effects result in lower costs as production increases.

Questions 12–14 refer to the map below.

Mercosur Membership

Legend

■ Full members

▧ Associate members

12. Mercosur is which of the following types of organizations?
    a. Customs union
    b. Environmental protection organization
    c. International lending agency
    d. Military alliance
    e. Supranational union

13. Based on the map, which of the following roles does geography likely play in the formation of Mercosur?
   a. South American countries sought a way to pool their considerable natural resources.
   b. Political rivalries are less likely to arise between neighboring states.
   c. Significant economic cooperation and coordination is possible between neighboring states.
   d. Regional countries are influenced by the same climatic conditions.
   e. Countries with the same site and situation are more likely to join a regional trade bloc.

14. Which of the following best explains how Mercosur benefits its member states?
   a. Mercosur leverages comparative advantage and allows member states to jointly negotiate trade deals.
   b. Mercosur increases political cooperation, and it created the foundation for a supranational state.
   c. Mercosur helps member states balance budgets and avoid financial crises, including debt crises.
   d. Mercosur provides national states with more control over national tariffs.
   e. Mercosur increases the efficiency of microloans and other strategies of development.

15. Which of the following best explains how economic development impacts gender parity?
   a. Economic development improves gender parity because it often results in wealth redistribution.
   b. Economic development decreases gender inequality by expanding educational and professional opportunities for women.
   c. Economic development has a marginal impact on gender parity because women primarily work in the agricultural sector.
   d. Economic development exacerbates gender inequality because it strengthens preexisting power structures.
   e. Economic development further marginalizes women, increasing the likelihood of women bearing the full burden of household responsibilities.

Answer Explanations

1. A: The photograph depicts Old Faithful Geyser in Yellowstone National Park, and the prompt mentions the commercialization of environmental features. Ecotourism is an economic activity in which people travel to relatively undisturbed locations in a natural environment, such as national parks. Choice *B* is incorrect because growth poles are economic sectors with higher rates of growth than the natural average. Choice *C* is incorrect because neoliberalism refers to policies related to free trade and free markets. Choice *D* is incorrect because outsourcing involves businesses moving jobs to overseas locations in order to reduce costs. Choice *E* is incorrect because ecotourism is a type of sustainable development, and the photograph specifically depicts a popular site of ecotourism.

2. D: The diagram features five boxes that are arranged in a vertical order, and the boxes' labels match concepts from Rostow's Stages of Economic Growth. In addition, the vertical arrangement of the boxes suggests a linear trajectory of economic development, which is consistent with Rostow's Stages of Economic Growth. Choice *A* is incorrect because the bid-rent theory asserts that profit motive acts as an organizing principle in regard to the arrangement of economic sectors in an urban environment. Choice *B* is incorrect because dependency theory contends that core countries exploit periphery countries, effectively undermining their economic development. Choice *C* is incorrect because New Urbanism relates to urban sustainability. Choice *E* is incorrect because Wallerstein's World Systems Theory classifies countries as either core, semi-periphery, or periphery countries in terms of economic development. In contrast, the diagram refers to how an individual country develops economically.

3. E: Western European countries have highly developed economies based on mass consumption and mass production, and they occupy a dominant role within the global economic system. Box 5 is the most advanced stage of economic development in this diagram. Choice *A* is incorrect because Box 1 is a traditional agricultural society, a stage that Western European countries surpassed several centuries ago. Choice *B* is incorrect because Box 2 refers to the preconditions for takeoff, such as the dissemination of technology and commercial agricultural production. Although Western European countries have retained these attributes, they have graduated from this stage of economic development. Choice *C* is incorrect because it's referring to the initial spread of urbanization and industrialization. Most Western European countries industrialized in the seventeenth and eighteenth centuries. Choice *D* is incorrect because Western European countries have also already successfully transitioned to developed status.

4. D: The Human Development Index (HDI) is used to rank countries based on their economic development and quality of life. The HDI has three key components—life expectancy at birth, mean and expected years of educational achievement, and per capita income. Choice *A* is incorrect because although civil liberties impact economic development and quality of life, it is not directly included in the calculation of HDI. Choice *B* is incorrect because although environmental sustainability refers to minimizing the destruction of natural ecosystems and avoiding the depletion of natural resources, this concept isn't directly related to the HDI. Choices *C* and *E* are incorrect because female empowerment and reproductive health are more closely associated with the Gender Inequality Index than the HDI.

5. C: The map labels countries as core countries, semi-periphery countries, or periphery countries. Wallerstein's World Systems Theory was the first model to organize countries' economic development in this way. Dependency theory uses the same three categorizes, but it adds an argument about how core countries have more advanced economies due to the exploitation of periphery countries' raw resources and workforce. Choices *A* and *B* are incorrect because the commodity dependence theory asserts that an overreliance on exporting commodities has a stifling effect on economic development, and it doesn't use the organizational scheme expressed on the map. Choices *D* and *E* are incorrect because Rostow's Stages of Economic Growth argues that countries develop economically in a linear fashion across five different stages. In addition, Rostow's Stages of Economic Growth doesn't use the concepts of core countries, semi-periphery countries, and periphery countries.

6. B: Core countries are defined by their large service sectors and specialization in high-end manufacturing, such as high-technology industries. In contrast, periphery countries are a source of cheap labor and raw resources within the global economic system's division of labor. Although it's somewhat incomplete, Choice *B* accurately expresses major differences between core countries and periphery countries. Choice *A* is incorrect because core countries don't exclusively specialize in high-technology industries. These countries have large service sectors and retain some blue-collar manufacturing industries. Choice *C* is incorrect because although core countries do have larger economies than periphery countries, there isn't typically a more equitable distribution of wealth in periphery countries. Often, income inequality is worse in periphery countries than core countries. Choice *D* is incorrect because core countries extract raw resources from periphery countries, but periphery countries aren't the primary beneficiaries of free-trade agreements. Core countries similarly benefit from free-trade agreements through the maximization of comparative advantage. Choice *E* is incorrect because there are several core countries outside of Western Europe, such as the United States, Canada, and Australia. In addition, there are a number of periphery countries in the Middle East and Africa.

7. D: The United Nations Development Programme has agreed to seventeen Sustainable Development Goals for 2030. These goals are highly ambitious, and they focus on strengthening countries in terms of social stability, economic development, and environmental sustainability. Although limiting the negative effects of gentrification would be included in several different Sustainable Development Goals, the United Nations Development Programme didn't specifically adopt preventing gentrification as a goal. Climate action (Choice *A*), ending poverty (Choice *B*), gender equality (Choice *C*), and sustainable urban development (Choice *E*) are incorrect because they are all Sustainable Development Goals for 2030.

8. E: The table provides data on the region's adjusted net income per capita. This data reflects the region's relative level of economic development. In other words, regions with the least economic development will have the lowest net income per capita. Based on the information provided in the table, the sub-Saharan African region ranks last in income per capita ($1,235). Choice *A* is incorrect because the European Union has the second highest income per capita ($28,096). Choice *B* is incorrect because the Latin America and Caribbean region has a significantly higher income per capita ($7,784) than sub-Saharan Africa. Similarly, Choice *C* is incorrect because the Middle East and North Africa also has a higher income per capita ($6,158) than sub-Saharan Africa. Choice *D* is incorrect because North America has the highest income per capita ($50,014).

9. E: Compared to semi-periphery countries and periphery countries, core countries have the most advanced economies and highest income per capita. The United States and Canada are both core countries, and they account for two of the three countries that are located in the North American region. This explains why North America has the highest income per capita by a considerable margin. Choice *A* is incorrect because although there are some special economic zones and export processing zones in North America, they are not the primary reason for this region's level of economic development. Special economic zones and export processing zones are more critical to the economic development of semi-periphery and periphery countries because they support an expansion of manufacturing jobs. Choice *B* is incorrect because although North America does have significant

amounts of natural resources, this is a more attenuated connection to economic development than Choice *E*. Deposits of natural resources don't necessarily result in economic development. Choice *C* is incorrect because although North American countries have extensive commercial links to the European Union, this isn't significantly different from other regions. The contemporary global economic system is based on interdependent commercial relationships. Likewise, Choice *D* is incorrect because nearly all countries have embraced neoliberalism since the fall of the Soviet Union in 1990.

10. B: Dependency theory asserts that core countries develop based on the exploitation of periphery countries' raw resources, lax environmental protections, and cheap labor. Accordingly, dependency theory believes this exploitation prevents periphery countries from developing economically. There are a handful of periphery countries in the South Asian region, such as Afghanistan, Bangladesh, and Pakistan. Choice *A* is incorrect because it states an explanation for stagnant economic development based on the theory of commodity dependence. Choice *C* is incorrect because subsistence agriculture is commonly practiced in South Asian countries due to systemic poverty, but dependency theory would argue that this is caused by core countries' exploitation of this region. Choice *D* is incorrect because although core countries have outsourced a significant number of manufacturing jobs to South Asia, this has arguably increased the region's income per capita. In any event, dependency theory doesn't believe outsourcing is the primary cause of economic stagnation. Choice *E* is incorrect because international lending agencies provide financial assistance to several South Asian countries, but the aid is not dependent on ecotourism. Additionally, dependency theory doesn't focus on ecotourism.

11. C: Multiplier effects refer to how some economic activities have a spillover effect, which benefits a variety of tangential economic sectors. For example, the construction of a new sports arena has a multiplier effect on the surrounding area because large crowds incentivize the establishment of more restaurants, bars, and other businesses. All of the other answer choices provide the definitions for different economic concepts. Choice *A* is incorrect because the physical concentration of businesses is known as *agglomeration*. Choice *B* is incorrect because post-Fordist methods of production increase flexibility in the manufacturing of specialized goods. Choice *D* is incorrect because the World Trade Organization is widely credited for establishing the regulatory framework for international trade. Choice *E* is incorrect because "economies of scale" is an economic principle stating that costs decrease as production increases.

12. A: The map provides a visual representation of Mercosur member states. Mercosur is a customs union intended to promote free trade between members. In addition, the customs union jointly negotiates trade policies, which increases the members' bargaining power. Choice *B* is incorrect because Mercosur is much more concerned with free trade and economic development than environmental protection. Choice *C* is incorrect because although many individual members of Mercosur have longstanding relationships with international lending agencies, such as the International Monetary Fund, Mercosur doesn't specialize in lending programs. Likewise, Choice *D* is incorrect because some of the members have entered into a military alliance, but Mercosur isn't directly related to those agreements. Choice *E* is incorrect because Mercosur doesn't feature a supranational government, meaning that member states are the sole sovereign authority within their territories.

13. C: Mercosur includes every country in South America, and therefore neighbors are jointly cooperating with this regional organization. Physical proximity facilitates economic cooperation and coordination. For example, neighboring states can easily share resources to be used in the implementation and enforcement of free-trade policies. If the members of Mercosur weren't neighboring states, it would have dramatically altered how Mercosur was formed and designed. Choice *A* is incorrect because Mercosur is a customs union, which doesn't require member states to pool natural resources. Choice *B* is incorrect because political rivalries frequently arise between neighboring states; in fact, there are numerous rivalries between Mercosur member states, such as the ongoing dispute between Venezuela and Brazil. Choice *D* is incorrect because South America is a relatively large region, and Mercosur extends across the entire continent. Consequently, the member states didn't develop under the same climatic conditions. Choice *E* is incorrect because Mercosur member states don't share the same site, which refers to a specific physical location.

14. A: Mercosur is primarily devoted to expanding free trade. Comparative advantage is the foundation for tree trade, and it increases economic efficiency by directing economic production toward goods with the lowest opportunity costs. Additionally, Mercosur increases member states' leverage in the negotiation of free-trade deals with foreign powers. Choice *B* is incorrect because a supranational state doesn't exist in South America. Choice *C* is incorrect because Mercosur isn't directly involved in balancing budgets. Many member states, particularly Argentina, have faced severe debt crises. Choice *D* is incorrect; Mercosur limits member states' control over national tariffs because they jointly negotiate trade deals with foreign powers. For example, if Mercosur signs a free-trade deal with China, Argentina cannot unilaterally impose tariffs on Chinese goods. Choice *E* is incorrect because Mercosur can increase the efficiency of economic development programs but only through its impact on free trade.

15. B: Economic development generally improves gender parity. Developing countries seek to expand educational and professional opportunities for women in order to strengthen their workforce and spur economic growth. For example, international organizations and national governments oversee microloan programs to support female entrepreneurs. Choice *A* is incorrect because economic development typically doesn't involve wealth redistribution; it occurs within the framework of a capitalist global economic system. Choice *C* is incorrect because although women continue to account for a significant percentage of the agricultural workforce in many developing countries, economic development tends to increase and diversify professional opportunities for women, resulting in more women working outside the agricultural sector. Choice *D* is incorrect because economic development is sometimes criticized for failing to address issues with preexisting power structures, but it rarely worsens gender inequality. Likewise, Choice *E* is incorrect because economic development reduces the marginalization of women, particularly through increasing the number of women who work outside the household in non-agricultural economic sectors.

Free Response Questions

Free Response Question 1

Countries vary in terms of economic development, but all countries exist within a relatively interdependent global economic system.

A. What are two strategies of economic development that seek to improve standards of living?

B. Explain the contemporary international division of labor in reference to the following THREE concepts.

- 1. Outsourcing
- 2. Special economic zones
- 3. Economic restructuring

C. Identify and describe ONE neoliberal policy in terms of its role in upholding the global economic system.

Sample Response

A. Two strategies of economic development that seek to improve standards of living are microloan programs and free-trade agreements. Microloan programs attempt to increase the role of women in economic development by directly providing female entrepreneurs with financial assistance. These programs improve standards of living by expanding employment opportunities for women and stimulating economic growth. In addition, microloans for women also benefit the standard of living for families because women are often the heads of households. Free-trade agreements remove barriers to international trade, such as tariffs and state subsidies for domestic industries. International trade can increase the efficiency of domestic production and create more employment opportunities. Furthermore, free-trade agreements can attract foreign investment for local businesses and state-sponsored development projects.

B. The contemporary international division of labor has been heavily influenced by outsourcing, special economic zones, and economic restructuring. Outsourcing refers to how businesses in core countries have transferred jobs overseas to reduce labor costs and exploit weaker environmental regulations. Many of these jobs have been in the blue-collar manufacturing sector. Businesses especially favor relocating to special economic zones, such as free-trade zones and export processing zones. In general, special economic zones have lower taxes and fewer trade restrictions than the rest of the country. In core countries, outsourcing has triggered large-scale economic restructuring. Most significantly, economies have been restructured through a collapse of industrial sectors and an expansion of the service sector. In effect, the service industry has replaced many of the jobs lost to outsourcing; however, a significant number of workers have struggled to make this transition.

C. The World Trade Organization (WTO) facilitates globalization by increasing free trade. This international organization was founded after the fall of the Soviet Union when capitalism emerged as the dominant global economic system. The WTO increases free trade in two ways. First, the WTO provides a legal and logistical framework for trade deals. States use this framework when negotiating trade deals. Second, the WTO offers a forum for dispute resolution. This forum helps preserve free-trade agreements by providing solutions other than termination. Overall, free trade has altered spatial relationships at different geographic scales. National economies have grown interdependent on the global economic system. Countries have also formed tighter regional bonds based on free-trade agreements, such as Mercosur in South America. Locally, businesses now compete in a global marketplace dominated by multinational corporations.

Free Response Question 2

Modern Combine Harvester

The combine harvester shown in the photograph is an example of how agricultural innovations have exponentially increased the global food supply; however, the contemporary agricultural system faces a number of challenges and controversies.

A. Explain how agricultural innovations led to the Green Revolution.

B. Explain ONE controversy related to each of the following THREE concepts.

- 1. Genetically modified organisms
- 2. Aquacultures
- 3. Food distribution

C. Identify TWO specific examples of land cover change caused by contemporary agricultural practices.

Sample Response

A. Agricultural innovations, such as high-yield crops and combined harvesters, directly led to the Green Revolution. During the latter half of the twentieth century, agricultural innovations increased the efficiency and effectiveness of agricultural production. Specifically, agricultural innovations facilitated the growth of large-scale agricultural operations, which have been the Green Revolution's lasting legacy. For example, combine harvesters allowed farmers to use larger tracts of farmland, and high-yield crops increased the amount of crops produced per square unit of land. Overall, the Green Revolution dramatically increased the global food supply, reducing malnutrition and the frequency of famines.

B. Genetically modified organisms, aquacultures, and inefficiencies in food distribution chains have been controversial. Genetically modified organisms are especially controversial because they have dramatically reduced the biodiversity of crops. Because there's significantly less variety in the types of crops being cultivated, an issue with a genetically modified organism could prove catastrophic. For example, if genetically modified corn failed, there could be a global shortage of corn because the vast majority of farmers are using the same type of corn. Aquacultures destroy coastal ecosystems through the introduction of antibiotics and invasive species. These by-products are difficult to avoid due to the fact that aquacultures require significant human intervention, largely because it's difficult to continually cultivate a population of fish that isn't native to the environment. Inefficiencies in food distribution can result in food deserts, or areas that lack access to sources of fresh food. Food deserts are most common in low-income communities because food distributors seek out locations with the greatest potential for profit. In both developed and developing countries, food deserts constitute a major cause of malnutrition.

C. Contemporary agricultural practices have resulted in deforestation and desertification. Large-scale agricultural and ranching operations have cleared massive amounts of forests to secure new sources of arable land and pastures. This deforestation results in land cover change because forest ecosystems are converted for agricultural purposes. Desertification occurs when agricultural production and/or livestock overexploit soil, resulting in a phenomenon known as "soil death." When the soil is totally depleted, it can result in the surrounding area turning into a desert. Furthermore, desertification can also occur when irrigation techniques and fertilizers increase salinity levels to such an extent that the soil can no longer support life.

Free Response Question 3

Polluted Canal in Montreal

Greater Tokyo Rapid Transit System

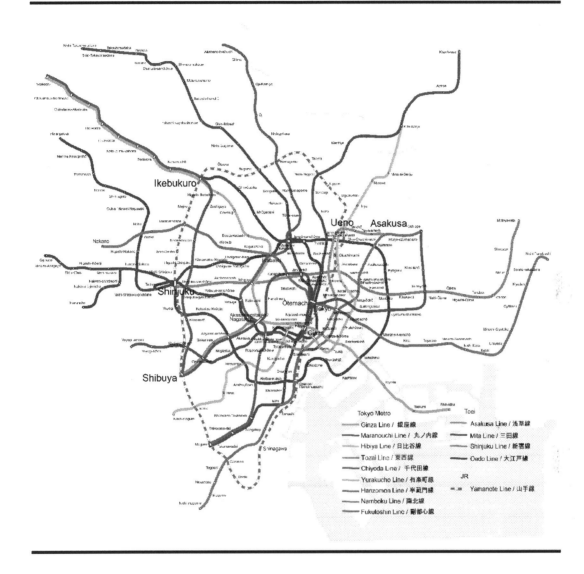

The photograph of a polluted canal and map of a transit system illustrate how urban development can create challenges that must be addressed in order to achieve sustainable economic growth.

A. For each of the following THREE categories, identify and explain ONE challenge created by urban development.

1. Economic
2. Social
3. Environmental

B. Explain how public transportation systems alter spatial relationships at different geographic scales.

C. Identify and explain ONE urban renewal initiative that directly addresses environmental harm.

Sample Response

A. Urban development creates economic, environmental, and social challenges. Cities often experience rapid population growth that results in a shortage of affordable housing. This shortage becomes increasingly problematic when residents are spending a disproportionate amount of their income on housing, which reduces inhabitants' disposable income. Additionally, housing shortages can lead to the development of squatter settlements, contributing to the spread of economic blight. Competitive housing markets also create social challenges. De facto segregation occurs when gentrification increases housing prices, displacing local residents. Property owners can also cause de facto segregation when they engage in redlining, which involves a refusal to sell or rent property to certain racial groups. Environmental pollution is a threat to quality of life, and it disproportionately impacts low-income communities. When environmental injustice reaches an intolerable level, it can transform low-income neighborhoods into zones of abandonment.

B. Public transportation systems alter spatial relationships at different geographic scales. At the local level, adequate access to public transportation can attract customers and allow residents to travel farther distances for work. Many cities encourage transportation-oriented development, which involves grouping commercial and residential developments around public transportation infrastructure. Public transportation networks can also deepen ties within an entire metropolitan region, connecting the urban core to outlying areas. For example, Tokyo's rapid transit system connects to a wide range of suburbs in the surrounding region. As a result, public transportation can mitigate the negative consequences of sprawl, such as traffic congestion and air pollution. On a national and international scale, passenger railroad services create networks and linkages, functioning as the connective tissue for an urban hierarchy. For example, Amtrak connects dozens of major cities in the United States and Canada. Similar railroad systems are also critical to strengthening the social and economic relationship between European Union member states.

C. The remediation and redevelopment of brownfields is an urban initiative that reduces urban pollution and increases environmental sustainability. Brownfields are urban areas that have been abandoned or heavily polluted. The remediation of brownfields involves removing pollutants, such as toxic chemicals and other forms of hazardous waste. Following remediation, the brownfields are often transformed into residential and commercial developments. Municipal administrations often include the remediation and redevelopment of brownfields in urban renewal projects because it raises property values in the surrounding area. Additionally, the redevelopment of brownfields enhances environmental sustainability because it increases the efficiency of land-use practices.

Dear AP Human Geography Test Taker,

We would like to start by thanking you for purchasing this study guide for your AP Human Geography exam. We hope that we exceeded your expectations.

Our goal in creating this study guide was to cover all of the topics that you will see on the test. We also strove to make our practice questions as similar as possible to what you will encounter on test day. With that being said, if you found something that you feel was not up to your standards, please send us an email and let us know.

We would also like to let you know about other books in our catalog that may interest you.

AP English Language and Composition

This can be found on Amazon: amazon.com/dp/162845928X

AP Chemistry

amazon.com/dp/1628456914

SAT

amazon.com/dp/1628456868

We have study guides in a wide variety of fields. If the one you are looking for isn't listed above, then try searching for it on Amazon or send us an email.

Thanks Again and Happy Testing!
Product Development Team
info@studyguideteam.com

FREE Test Taking Tips DVD Offer

To help us better serve you, we have developed a Test Taking Tips DVD that we would like to give you for FREE. **This DVD covers world-class test taking tips that you can use to be even more successful when you are taking your test.**

All that we ask is that you email us your feedback about your study guide. Please let us know what you thought about it – whether that is good, bad or indifferent.

To get your **FREE Test Taking Tips DVD**, email freedvd@studyguideteam.com with "FREE DVD" in the subject line and the following information in the body of the email:

a. The title of your study guide.

b. Your product rating on a scale of 1-5, with 5 being the highest rating.

c. Your feedback about the study guide. What did you think of it?

d. Your full name and shipping address to send your free DVD.

If you have any questions or concerns, please don't hesitate to contact us at freedvd@studyguideteam.com.

Thanks again!

Made in the USA
Coppell, TX
05 August 2021